**Citizen Involvement in
Crime Prevention**

# Citizen Involvement in Crime Prevention

George J. Washnis
Center for Governmental Studies

Lexington Books
D.C. Heath and Company
Lexington, Massachusetts
Toronto          London

**Library of Congress Cataloging in Publication Data**

Washnis, George J.
    Citizen involvement in crime prevention.

    1. Crime prevention—Citizen participation—
Case studies. 2. Public relations—Police—Case
studies. 3. Crime prevention—United States.
I. Title.
HV7431.W37            364.4'4            75-5238
ISBN 0-669-99812-5

Published simultaneously in Canada.

Second printing, March 1977.

Printed in the United States of America.

International Standard Book Number: 0-669-99812-5

Library of Congress Catalog Card Number: 75-5238

# Contents

# Foreword

Urban dwellers everywhere are concerned with personal safety and with protection of their property. Crime is one of their gravest worries. In response, police forces have expanded, have applied new technology, and have purchased new kinds of hardware. Yet, crime continues unabated.

We are now beginning to see that it is too much to expect the police department to do the job alone. There must be improvement in the courts and in the correctional system. There must be efforts at eliminating the underlying causes of crime, such as unemployment, poverty, racial discrimination, rootlessness, alienation. Above all, members of the community must play larger roles in crime prevention.

Indeed, greater community involvement is happening in many cities around the country. Organized neighborhood associations and other community groups are mobilizing to halt the on-rush of crime, to promote personal safety, to restore order. Working in partnership with the police, many such groups are making headway in crime prevention.

This experience forms the basis for this book. George Washnis presents the findings of a study undertaken by the Center for Governmental Studies with financing from the National Institute of Law Enforcement and Criminal Justice (grant number 74-TA-99-1009), authorized under the Omnibus Crime Control and Safe Streets Act of 1968. Because of the wide range of matters involving citizens in law enforcement and the thousands of projects underway, the Center decided to concentrate on police-community projects where citizens were actively involved and largely independent of government control. These groups, however, were ones which work in close cooperation with police. Some 37 projects were reviewed in seventeen cities, and a national survey was also conducted to determine which cities had the most meaningful programs. A 100 percent completion was obtained through questionnaires and phone inquiries of the 100 largest cities. In addition, the opinions of block leaders were sampled in three cities in regard to crime and fear and efficacy of the local program.

For this study the Center's staff included George J. Washnis, project director, Dr. John Florer, associate researcher, and Ronald Cooper, student intern. Valuable work was done by the following field consultants: Keith Bennett, Knoxville, Tennessee; Ellen Filurin, Chicago, Illinois; Kenneth Hansen, Los Angeles, California; James Hetherington, Indianapolis, Indiana; Mark Kent, Mobile, Alabama; Ron Lawrence, St. Louis, Missouri; Lawrence Resnick, New York, New York; and Terhan Shabaze, Braddock, Pennsylvania. Much thanks goes to Clementine Taylor who performed typing, scheduling, and administrative chores, to Caroline Taylor for typing, and to Maureen Lynch Edison and Thomas Goldwasser for editing.

Members of the Center's board made valuable contributions in reviewing and offering comments on the report, as did the staff of the National Institute of Law Enforcement and Criminal Justice. Particular credit is given to members of a special review panel who spent a good deal of time in reviewing the work and who made excellent suggestions and recommendations. The panel included the following persons: Thomas W. Cochee, Chief of Police, Compton, California; Eugene Denton, Assistant City Manager, Dallas, Texas; Donald McElvoy, Director, National Conference of Christians and Jews, New York City; Ross Flanagan of the Block Association of West Philadelphia, Philadelphia, Pennsylvania; Robert McCann, Lieutenant, Chicago Police Department, Chicago, Illinois.

We hope this study demonstrates to both community groups and police officials which type of police-community crime prevention projects can be successful as well as encouraging them to implement many of them in their own communities.

It goes without saying that any opinions, findings, conclusions, or recommendations expressed herein are those of the author and do not necessarily reflect the views of the Institute, the Law Enforcement Assistance Administration, or the Department of Justice.

Howard W. Hallman
President
Center for Governmental Studies

*Washington, D.C.*
*September 1975*

**Citizen Involvement in
Crime Prevention**

# 1 Citizen Involvement in Crime Prevention

## Introduction

More than in any past years, police officials and criminologists believe that active and serious citizen involvement is essential if crime is to be substantially reduced. Out of necessity the general public has been stimulated to assist undermanned, overtaxed, and often non-community-oriented police forces in the development of healthy and secure neighborhoods. However, considerable uncertainty exists about the extent to which the public should be involved, about what the public is capable of doing, and about the degree to which public participation can affect the reduction of crime and fear. Without reliable analytical data, uncertainties like these are difficult to resolve. But surveys and experiences are available which present a fairly accurate overview and assess results of citizen involvement as it now operates. Here we describe multiple ways in which citizens assist police and ways in which police cooperate and work with citizens, as well as the successes and shortcomings of these efforts.

### Focus

Specifically, this book concentrates on citizens working with police. It does not review other elements in the criminal justice system, such as courts, probation, or corrections, except incidentally. Community-police activities are assessed where private citizens either have taken the initiative to start them or have largely operated them on their own; police-initiated projects are reviewed also for those cases in which citizens play an active part and exercise some independence. Police-controlled programs — projects where police supervise participants entirely, establish all the rules and regulations, or provide all the resources — are not of primary importance here. Community Service Officers and other police-paid or uniformed civilian personnel are discussed only as parts of a total crime prevention system. Our attention is devoted to citizens, mostly volunteers, who use limited funds and run their own operations but in cooperation with the police.

### Nature of Activities

Some of the activities have a familiar ring — block clubs, neighborhood watch, whistle stop, operation identification, anticrime crusades, "eyes and ears" of the police, police-community councils, neighborhood walks, mobile patrols, and other related projects. City and police officials want to know whether these programs are merely gimmicks or actually contribute to crime reduction. This book answers these questions through several methods, which include direct observation of projects, analysis of crime statistics, surveys, and assessments by local officials. Effective use of these findings and suggested prototypes should help save time for police officials and help them to avoid unnecessary additional experimentation. Hopefully this material, which is designed for use by police and resident groups, will motivate both local officials and citizens to initiate similar programs.

To achieve success, it normally makes little difference whether police or residents initiate a project as long as both groups agree on basic principles, methods of operation, and how to maintain and equitably administer a program. Both police and residents strongly desire a reduction in crime and fear; both want liberties preserved and justice served.

In effective citizen involvement, vigilantism is not tolerated, although a small fraction of concerned citizens have sometimes tried to take the law into their own hands. With few exceptions, community groups cooperate well with police, carry no weapons, and perform mainly as eyes and ears for sworn officials. Citizens engage in projects that are preventive and peaceful in nature, as well as active crime prevention surveillance and ambitious lobbying for law enforcement legislation and improved services. Citizen involvement includes patrolling, taking pictures of offenders, and using whistles, horns, and sometimes verbal admonishment to discourage and scare off criminals.

*Racial Mix*

Mostly white, middle-income groups are active in community crime prevention projects; however, in many areas the poor are involved, and in some cities just as many blacks as whites participate. In many neighborhoods blacks suffer a higher rate of crime and injustice than whites and are certainly just as concerned.

Most communities have made strong efforts for racial and ethnic mix in participation. Largely reflective of the existing characteristics of each neighborhood, hundreds of all-white, all-black, and mixed racial groups operate. In some areas, black groups have been as easily organized as white. For example, Chicago has a number of all-black citizen patrols which organized of their own volition. Oakland and New York City have many all-black block clubs because that is the make-up of the neighborhood. These and most of the other cities in this report also have a large percentage of block clubs which are racially mixed.

In largely mixed racial communities, whites generally seem to have more fear of crime than blacks. But in the nearly all-white or all-black neighborhoods, fear seems to be at an equally high level for all races. Race and ethnicity seem to make no difference when it comes to the desire to reduce crime. And where signs of vigilantism appear, they come with equal force in black and white communities. Fortunately, police officials have been able to stop most such attempts and to guide groups in constructive directions.

## Economic Factors

Perhaps economic differences are more significant than racial ones in terms of gaining community interest. It appears more difficult to organize and maintain low-income groups than middle-income ones. The latter — usually homeowners concerned about property values and with a high degree of community pride — are naturally inclined to be protective of their neighborhood and more willing to organize to guard it. On the other hand, it is often more difficult to organize higher-income communities because residents usually have proved successful in demanding and getting better police protection. Also these income groups are more likely to live in neighborhoods distant from the major or more violent criminal element. However, more and more crime prevention groups are being formed in wealthy sections of town and in low-income and public housing projects. In more stable areas where preservation of the neighborhood is honored, police usually take a deeper interest than in other areas, and they engage in intensive campaigns to get residents to secure their homes, identify properties, and perform as the "eyes and ears" for police.

Preferably, police campaigns should be oriented citywide. Emphasis naturally varies, depending on community interest and the extent of the crime problem. Furthermore, block associations are more likely to retain their viability when the racial, ethnic, and income groups of the particular community where they operate are balanced and all residents are encouraged to participate.

## Evaluation Methods and Cities Reviewed

Documenting actual reduction in crime as the result of community crime prevention efforts is difficult. Many factors affect the crime rate, such as unemployment, illiteracy, poverty, drug abuse, boredom, discrimination, and alienation. However, when crime rates fall, many persons are ready to take credit. Explanations for improvement may cover such things as more police, improved security techniques, better courts and corrections, change in economic and social conditions, active community involvement, and various other matters. For evidence of crime reduction from community involvement, expert opinions of police officials and impressions of block leaders and residents were used here. Surveys of block leaders were also conducted in three cities and projects observed first-hand. Several hundred block leaders in Philadelphia, Oakland, and Compton were surveyed to determine whether block captains believe block club organization has helped to reduce crime and fear in their neighborhoods. The results of these surveys appear in Chapter 4.

Staff and consultants made field visits and reviewed thirty-six projects in seventeen cities, which included the following:

| City | Project |
|------|---------|
| New York, New York | Block clubs, mobile and taxi patrols, high-rise security, maintenance employees safety, parent safety leagues, community councils, private funding sources |
| Philadelphia, Pennsylvania | Block clubs, mobile patrols, community councils |
| Chicago, Illinois | Block clubs, mobile patrols, and civilian radio patrols |
| Los Angeles, California | Block clubs and civilian radio patrols |
| Compton, California | Block clubs and civilian radio patrols |
| San Jose, California | Community councils |
| Okaland, California | Block clubs and community councils |
| East Palo Alto, California | Youth involvement and youth councils |
| Mobile, Alabama | Block clubs and mobile patrols |
| Knoxville, Tennessee | Block clubs and mobile patrols |
| Braddock, North Braddock, and Rankin, Pennsylvania | Youth patrols |
| Dallas, Texas | Civilian beat committees |
| Minneapolis, Minnesota | Block clubs and community councils |
| St. Paul, Minnesota | Property identification |
| Simi Valley, California | Community councils and administrative counseling |
| St. Louis, Missouri | Anticrime crusade |
| Indianapolis, Indiana | Anticrime crusade |

A mail and phone survey of community crime prevention projects in the 100 largest cities (100 percent response) and a sampling of medium- and smaller-sized cities were also conducted.

## Book Outline

We sampled citizen involvement in a variety of police and community activities. The first review is citizen block associations, which perform as the eyes and ears for the police department and engage in home security, walking patrols, and related activities. Second, we discuss the success or failure of different kinds of mobile patrols. The third category describes special projects involving high-rise security, employee and child safety, youth and taxi patrols, and uniformed and paid civilian forces. The fourth area of discussion is police-community councils, methods of operation, and degree of acceptance by police. The fifth review group is citywide anticrime crusades and their purposes and relationships to block associations and community councils. In addition, we discuss the methods and desirability of private funding to assist police departments. Finally, the elements of a crime prevention plan for police departments are outlined, and ways are suggested to implement these concepts in both large and small cities and counties.

Some projects appear to fall between categories. However, several of these are closely related to the block association concept. For example, security projects operated by tenant associations in high-rise buildings perform much like street-level block groups. Protective organizations for nighttime maintenance employees are different in some respects yet have many similarities to other crime-fighting groups. Some mobile patrols operate in special ways. A New York City taxi group operates on the same principle as neighborhood mobile patrols. Although there are differences, most citizen efforts resemble each other in tactics and purpose.

Often gaps exist in programming between the use of sworn officers and neighborhood volunteers. These can be filled by using more highly supervised groups, such as community service officers, paid civilian employees, auxiliary police, and paraprofessionals. Each city and county must assess its own needs in order to develop a comprehensive prevention system which can effectively utilize sworn officers, civilian employees, and volunteers.[a]

*The Anticrime Search*

Community involvement is a necessary crime prevention ingredient. Police manpower, computers, better equipment, and new police techniques are not the total police answer to reducing crime. In fact, even with this emphasis crime has been consistently increasing. FBI figures show that during the last decade (1960-1970) the nation experienced a 176 percent rise in major crime, including a 76 percent increase in murders and manslaughter and a 224 percent increase in robberies. In 1974 alone, major crime increased over 12 percent nationally

---

[a]Information on the potential of civilian employees is presented in a forthcoming monograph, *Employing Civilians in Police Work,* prepared by the Urban Institute and funded by the National Institute of Law Enforcement and Criminal Justice.

and in the second quarter of 1975 increased 18 percent.[b] Expanded social consciousness and community awareness can be important factors in helping to reverse this trend. Many chiefs of police and their staffs are now actively encouraging community involvement as a necessary part of the anticrime answer. Also a growing number of citizens feel they can make a contribution by forming crime prevention associations on their own initiative. It is worth examining the process and techniques which have already developed.

## Summary

Thousands of block clubs and hundreds of mobile patrols are operating in many small American cities and counties. More and more municipalities are forming community groups and showing citizens how to get actively involved in fighting crime and assisting police. The trend is encouraging and should be stimulated. It is in these well-organized blocks where local police officials and residents have demonstrated that crime has been substantially reduced, while crime rates have been climbing citywide. Greater cooperation and understanding are needed between police and citizens, and as many neighborhoods and blocks as possible should be organized against crime.

---

[b]*Uniform Crime Reports for the United States,* Federal Bureau of Investigation, U.S. Department of Justice, Washington, D.C., 1970, 1972, 1974, 1975 (includes annual as well as quarterly reports).

# 2

## Block Associations

### The Reason for Block Clubs

Block associations are the natural product of a number of factors. These include the adverse experiences and provocations of the victims of crime, the general fear of crime, dissatisfaction with law enforcement and the criminal justice system, and the desperate feeling by some citizens that they have got to get actively involved in order to force crime down. The need for citizen participation is made more apparent when one considers that police performance is largely influenced by the degree citizens are themselves concerned and insistent on quality service. If residents show little interest in the life of their community, in its condition and safety and sense of well-being, police may wonder why they should care. Of course, police are paid to perform, yet too often their jobs are routine and uninteresting, and some officers believe they are not paid enough. Often active and constructive citizen involvement has resulted in increased police effectiveness and reduced crime rates — an important justification for the creation of block associations.

Several principal reasons lead the list of pros for block club organization. One is to increase communication and understanding between citizens and law enforcement officers so that police are motivated into doing a better job and residents into assisting them. Second is to reduce crime by making it more difficult for criminals to operate in a particular area due to the increased eyes and ears available to the police. A third reason is to develop a sense of community and comradeship among the residents, with a consequential reduction in the fear of crime.

### Motivates Police and Reduces Crime

Police officers possess a genuine desire to help citizens who help them. Obviously, motivating police and increasing their effectiveness can help to reduce crime. In city after city, the active involvement of block clubs has helped to improve police performance and reduce crime.

Although the law enforcement officer's job theoretically includes treating all law-abiding citizens equally, responding to calls with diligence, and spending nearly equal numbers of hours patrolling similar crime areas, not enough sworn officers are available, and other resources are limited.

7

Residents have a tendency to increase police interest in a neighborhood when they become organized, know beat officers by name, and assist police by calling in crimes and providing them with leads. Simple coffee klatches and block association meetings with both residents and police help to foster a spirit of cooperation. Communicating on the street level and by phone helps to draw police and residents together. Community walks and mobile patrols, home security, property identification, and numerous special projects have all helped to improve police responsiveness and interest in particular neighborhoods because of increased contact and understanding between residents and police.

Increased police response in well-organized neighborhoods does not necessarily mean that less attention is paid to unorganized areas. Police officials recognize that they have the responsibility to treat areas with similar crime characteristics in approximately the same manner. Usually, equal numbers of police and manhours are directed to similar areas. However, differences in the level of service occur because of how much interest officers take in their work. Community organization can make the difference between simple police coverage and active police involvement.

### Increases Police Response to Block Clubs

The number of block associations in each city gives some idea of areas which may be getting increased police response. In Oakland, for example, there are 900 functioning block associations. Over 3,000 operate in both New York City and Los Angeles, 31 in Compton, California, over 100 in Philadelphia, and dozens in Chicago, Mobile, Knoxville, and other cities. In some cities both residents and police officials say that certain blocks are getting more attention and service than others because organized residents communicate more effectively and demand better response.

### Makes Police Job Easier

Other benefits accrue. Part of the police job is communicating with residents, determining neighborhood problems, and establishing reliable two-way information links. Block clubs assist in these efforts; they also make the law enforcement job easier because police do not have to spend as much of their resources organizing citizens or finding cooperative witnesses to provide identification and information. Police enjoy working in communities where citizens are attempting to help them rather than where they refuse to cooperate. Too often citizens have stood by watching a "mugging" or other criminal act without helping the victim directly or even calling for assistance. Block clubs are one of the most valuable sources for training and alerting residents on how to become actively involved in assisting victims, summoning police, and serving as witnesses. Participation becomes a habit with many block club members and a duty for some.

## Improves Sense of Community

In regard to developing a sense of community, block associations have been one of the most effective ways of bringing people together. In city after city, the majority of block members report that they had never known most of their neighbors and that only through the block club coffee sessions and regular meetings and the door-to-door contact had they really gotten to know each other and to appreciate mutual problems. In many cases, prior to block organizing, even neighbors next door to each other communicated infrequently. Crime prevention provided the motivation to get together, and block associations offered the mechanism for doing it. The simple factor of adults and youth knowing each other has helped to reduce fear. Familiarity has developed friendly attitudes and an increased concern for one's neighborhood.

## Starting Block Clubs

### The Nature of Block Clubs

Perhaps the most important principle to consider is the nature of the block organization. Specifically its methods should involve nonviolence, no weapons, and an absence of vigilantism. Members should not intervene physically against crimes or use force. The police department should be notified early that the association is being formed to assist police, not to investigate or harass them. The latter role may be played by other organizations but not for the purposes described here. In several instances police cooperation has failed miserably because police were unsure of citizen motives. Community groups should make their motives absolutely clear.

### Private Initiative

Block clubs can be organized either by citizens themselves or by police. If citizens become sufficiently aroused by serious crime in their neighborhood, they and often the victim of crime may decide to organize a crime prevention group. In addition, anticrime crusades and police-community councils should support the creation of anticrime block clubs as a goal. In some cases, a neighborhood improvement association, church, or fraternal or civic group takes the initiative to organize clubs because of alarming and increasing crime rates.

Existing organizations should take a serious look at what they can do about crime in their community. If no organization is interested in working with the problem, private individual or police leadership must work on the issue.

In any case, the ways to organize a block club are outlined below:

1. An existing organization should bring the subject up at its next meeting; or an individual organizer should knock on doors, hand out leaflets, and call a neighborhood meeting.
2. The organization should seek the assistance of the police chief or his or her community relations head. It is important that police participation and understanding be gained from the outset.
3. The first meeting agenda should include a discussion of the crime problem in the neighborhood, the number and kinds of local victims, official police crime statistics, police policy and performance in dealing with neighborhood crime, presentation of instructive community experiences and case histories, and a general overview of crime problems and prevention techniques presented by a police official. Future agenda should include many of these same items.
4. During meetings, suggestions should be given for helping to correct problems, crime prevention pamphlets and other material distributed, and case histories presented concerning success or failure of organizations in other cities. The need for citizen involvement and its effect on reducing crime should be stressed.
5. Residents should be asked to sign up for participation and to solicit the membership of at least one other neighbor.
6. The method for recruiting members is important. Potential and new members must be assured that their privacy will not be invaded. Ample time should be provided for the initial sharing of each other's problems, experiences, fears, and solutions. Leaders must realize that they cannot arrive at abolute answers for all problems. They should strive to remain flexible enough to meet each contingency as it arises.
7. Basic committees should be established on rules and regulations, bylaws, new membership, programs, and special matters related to each neighborhood.
8. The purposes and objectives of the block club should be clearly enumerated. These may include the following items:
   a. Assist police by adding to their "eyes and ears."
   b. Encourage citizens to come forth as witnesses.
   c. Help police to identify and register household property.
   d. Motivate police and improve police service and productivity.
   e. Disseminate crime prevention pamphlets and newsletters.
   f. Advise residents about home security techniques, better locks, alarms, and other devices.

*g.* Inform the neighborhood about area conditions and solutions to problems.

*h.* Hold workshops on standards of conduct and sense of neighborliness.

*i.* Engage in projects especially designed for each neighborhood.

*j.* Assist the victims of crime and help in their readjustment.

## Police Initiative and Organization

When citizens do not assume the responsibility to learn about the crime problem and help to reduce it, police officials must.

Police departments should be especially staffed, and in the case of larger departments, special units should be established to organize and maintain relationships with citizens. For smaller departments, an officer should be assigned this responsibility even if only on a part-time basis.

## Locating Police Responsibility for Citizen Involvement

The responsibility for organizing and maintaining citizen participation has normally fallen with police community relations divisions or their equivalent. Some cities have found it preferable to locate this function directly under the patrol division in order to influence the beat police officer directly. There seems to be no single best method. Success or failure can occur either way. Much depends on the will, genuine belief, and leadership of the heads of these divisions; and conditions vary from city to city.

If the head of patrol, for example, possesses no appreciation for or declines to become familiar with citizen involvement, it can be disastrous to place this responsibility under him or her. Whether this function is placed under patrol or community relations, the chief of police must exert strong leadership, directing beat patrol officers' involvement with block clubs and community councils.

In some cases, officers from community relations — usually more attuned and knowledgeable about citizen involvement — with the support of the chief of police and other city officials, are able to motivate patrol officers even though the head of patrol may not be entirely sympathetic. As such, citizen involvement programs would be better located under such a unit.

Location of the community involvement function will have to be assessed and decided by each community. However, in large departments a distinct unit — either under patrol or community relations — should be established and assigned the responsibility for organizing new block units and helping to sustain existing ones. Their charge should include training, public relations, television and other communication media publicity, evaluation of block club and community council effectiveness, and transferring experiences. They should also inform the entire police department about the nature, success, or failure of various citizen involvement projects. Police training in these relatively new community involvement techniques should take place in the police academy as well as in periodic sessions at daily roll call.

**Beat Patrol Officers versus Central Units.** Police contact with citizens should preferably be conducted by the police officer on the beat. Police public relations units or similar divisions can serve well-defined purposes, but they should not be used as substitutes for regular patrol police contact. Central staff are ideally suited to evaluate and monitor programs; to train groups of block leaders; to prepare newsletters, pamphlets visual aides, and other material; to arrange for block award presentations and lectures; and to perform many functions to help organize and sustain citizen participation and other crime prevention programs. However, one should never lose sight of the importance of direct citizen contact by all patrol officers.

Residents are primarily interested in communicating with patrol officers assigned to their block and reviewing crime problems in the immediate neighborhood. Considerably less concern is shown for citywide crime rates or how effectively the police department assesses its overall performance. Indeed, they are interested in practical steps on how to reduce crime on their own blocks; they want to know the first names of the officers assigned there and be able to influence them to respond faster and more effectively.

An important by-product of direct contact is that beat patrol officers and block residents get to know each other better, so that friendship ensues and respect grows. Police officers are much more inclined to respond to and be interested in citizens whom they know well.

## Maintaining Block Clubs

One of the main difficulties with volunteer crime prevention groups is maintaining their viability. Many groups start out enthusiastically, but as crime recedes on their block or in the area, they tend to lose interest. Members usually remain seriously concerned about crime and fear but lose the will to attend meetings or to work actively for their association. This, however, is not the case for all groups. Some remain active for many years.

### The Importance of Leadership

More than anything else, block club viability depends on the strength and personal qualities of block leaders. A good leader, vitally interested in the neighborhood, can hold most groups together and motivate them in fulfilling certain agreed-upon objectives. It is easier to do this when crime is high and victims, who have been hurt by crime or discouraged with the law enforcement process, are plentiful. Victims are usually the best source for membership and also tend to remain members the longest.

In some cities, leaders have spread their skills to other blocks by training new block leaders. Some also have groomed a second echelon of leaders in case the initial organizers drop out or become disinterested. Sometimes loss of a single block leader can be disastrous to a club. Having someone available to fill leadership gaps is extremely important.

*Effective Number of Block Clubs*

If too many block clubs exist, they become difficult to sustain. Ideally, neighborhood improvement organizations and block clubs should be created in all parts of the city; however, without proper resources and central direction, many clubs have difficulty sustaining themselves. If police resources in workforce, communications, information dissemination, training, lecturing, and other assistance are spread too thin, some groups will not be serviced properly, nor can police response time be highly efficient in all areas. It is best for a jurisdiction to start small, develop a few highly successful block units where citizens are highly motivated, and expand gradually to the rest of the city. No block should be discouraged from organizing itself.

As long as sufficient police and volunteer workers are assigned to work with block clubs, the number of clubs which can be effectively maintained is not limited. Over 3,000 block clubs operate in both Los Angeles and New York City. The latter largely depends on its matching fund program to support club longevity, while Los Angeles relies on strong leadership and support from the chief of police and the direct assignment of beat patrol officers to this responsibility. Philadelphia's program is being expanded. It will be interesting to learn whether the city's civilian leaders can adequately train additional block and district leaders or themselves maintain the viability of new clubs. Oakland, for example, has experienced difficulties in maintaining its high level of block club participation; the number of clubs dropped from about 1,400 to 900. More recently, however, through renewed police department activity, the number is again rising. Smaller cities, with many fewer clubs, experience similar problems. Constant vigilence and injection of adequate resources are necessary to sustain them.

*Techniques for Maintaining Block Clubs*

Some essential techniques on how to maintain block club viability are listed below:

1. *Formal structure.* A citywide block club program needs a formal structure supported by a budget and police and civilian staffs to oversee operations. The simple movement of a beat or district leader from one area could cause collapse of many units unless permanent staff can fill in and recruit new leadership. The police department should have a special unit to work with and help maintain block clubs and community involvement. The appointment of civilian district and beat leaders will at least ensure that someone is prepared to deal with problems in any block under their jurisdiction in the absence of individual block leadership.

2. *Training.* Leaders need to be trained formally and in depth; and secondary and lower echelons should also be trained.

3. *Deputy leaders.* Each district leader should have a well-trained beat leader as an assistant or second-in-command who could readily replace the top person, if necessary. Too often when the original block captain moves from the neighborhood, the block club falls apart. Thus, the importance of an interested and active deputy cannot be overemphasized.

4. *District meetings.* District civilian leaders should meet at least quarterly to discuss problems from a citywide perspective.

5. *Workshops.* Workshops for district, beat, and block club leaders should be held to discuss new techniques and policies and to exchange information.

6. *Awards.* An annual awards dinner should be held to honor outstanding block leaders and police officers in the program. Citizens should be presented awards for making unusual contributions to the success of the program or for outstanding arrests or assistance to police.

7. *Broad agenda.* Crime prevention block clubs should eventually broaden their agenda to include other neighborhood improvement items, such as housing rehabilitation, beautification, parks and recreation development, street lighting, and bettering of other city services. As crime recedes on the block, solving these other important issues will help maintain interest in the association and serve as a reason for continuing to function. Crime prevention alone can become monotonous and myopic. Citizens are generally concerned about the total quality of living and want to take up those issues which are most important and timely. Block leaders must recognize the priority of issues and plan around them. At all times, crime prevention should be a significant part of the agenda.

8. *Promotion.* The mayor, city council, and other key city officials periodically need to boost the block club concept. Some city funds should be budgeted to publicize the program, for pamphlets and other communications media. Through public announcements and speeches, officials should inform as many residents of the community as possible

about the purpose and significance of community involvement. There should be room in the mayor's State of the City Message for mention of this program.

9. *Police endorsement.* The chief of police should explain the block club program through official police department memorandum and issue clear directives as to how police are to involve themselves, meet citizens, help organize block clubs, and respond to block club members. The details of this involvement should be part of the police department's regular training program taught at the academy and during daily roll call. Police department leadership must be genuine and continuous.

10. *Grants and matching funds.* Annual grants or matching funds to blocks will encourage continued activity. A city Guidelines Board to establish rules and amounts of matching funds is also valuable.

11. *False sense of security and lower crime rates.* A false sense of security can also harm community participation. Helicopters hovering about, greater police workforce, stringent sentences, and lower crime statistics all tend to pacify residents and lower their activity. The continued value of citizen vigilance must be stressed as a need above and beyond technical measures.

12. *Community pride.* Community pride is one of the main reasons people stick together and are willing to devote time to neighborhood improvement. This pride develops through a variety of sources including decent housing, good city services, acceptable environment, as well as a low crime rate. When neighbors get to know each other well and city officials pay attention to a particular neighborhood or block, pride expands further and residents are more willing to meet and work together over a long period of time.

13. *Related police functions.* Well-organized block clubs can be of invaluable assistance to special police programs. Team policing, police neighborhood action programs, and a host of other community involvement projects can be readily assisted by existing block groups which the police can plug into to make police jobs easier. The relatively new police-citizen involvement techniques should find ongoing and responsible citizen action of great value and will most likely extend the life of block organizations as one tends to depend on the other.

## Case Histories of Block Clubs

Numerous interesting citizen crime programs operate around the country. A review of a few case histories is worthwhile, beginning with Philadelphia, which is noted for its community walks; Oakland, for a citywide crime prevention committee which oversees the block program; Los Angeles, which has a greater number of clubs and receives high praise from the chief of police; Compton and its unusual crime conditions; and New York City, which subsidizes the block program.

## Block Association of West Philadelphia

Encompasssing tree-lined streets with old two-story buildings around the University of Pennsylvania, the Block Association of West Philadelphia (BAWP) was formed following a spate of crimes during the Christmas season of 1971. Robberies, muggings, burglaries, and rapes frightened and angered the community. Families found their living rooms empty of gifts and appliances when they returned from communion with their friends. The Happy New Year brought three rapes in two weeks. Certainly, isolating oneself at home was not the answer. What West Philadelphia did is typical of what many other groups have done across the nation.

A local minister's wife, Ellie Wegener, and a pacifist Quaker, Ross Flanagan, suggested a nonviolent response through the formation of active block associations. The program which resulted has been well received, crime has receded, and a sense of community among local residents has emerged. Now other sections of Philadelphia are following this lead, and the governor's Criminal Justice Commission is interested in expanding the concept statewide.

**Activities.** The basic plan, which began to take shape early in 1972, was to organize every block in an entire area. Now neighbors on each block meet monthly to review techniques of how to watch each other's homes and to exchange information on home security as well as new hardware and other related items.

Complete cooperation with the police has always been maintained. If a neighbor notices that a friend's house is being burglarized, she or he either telephones the police directly or contacts the block leader, who in turn calls the police. The association participants do not attempt to intervene physically against crimes or to use force. They act simply as eyes and ears.

The plan also involves security in the streets. Community walks are the prime volunteer resource and are used to scout for potential lawbreakers roaming the streets. Residents also make use of ear-splitting freon horns when danger seems imminent. Loud, piercing noise from the horns has scared off many a would-be attacker as well as alerting neighbors that immediate help is needed. When a resident hears a horn or spots trouble, he or she is instructed to go to the window and set off his or her own horn, call the police, turn on lights, and continue to make noise and to offer assistance when able.

Freon horns are more reliable than battery-powered devices, and, most significantly, are usually superior to whistles because many times victims are frightened and short of breath when under attack and therefore are unable to blow a whistle. Furthermore, whistles are too easily available. Almost every "kid on a bike" has one now, so they begin to lose their effect as a result of the "cry wolf once too often" syndrome. Under Philadelphia's program, the manufacturer agreed to limit freon horn sales to adults and crime prevention groups. They are not given to anyone until that person is well versed in their use. They are also not indiscriminately sold at bazaars and parties.

Block associations exchange information and ideas. When community workshops are held to share ideas, issues besides crime are discussed. For example, general community improvement and victim rehabilitation get a great deal of attention.

One important kind of information for volunteers involves how to patrol so as not to be mistaken for an offender. Mistaken identity could easily occur as one peruses the streets searching for potential lawbreakers. By patrolling only the streets, community walkers minimize their risk. Back yards and alleys, where movements would be more suspicious, are avoided.

**Organization.** From the beginning, financial resources have been limited. The two coordinators, Wegener and Flanagan, serve full time but with limited compensation. A recent LEAA grant of $27,000 provides part of their salaries and other expenses. These funds are used for expanding the block association concept to other areas and training new block leaders. Some private funds are also available.

BAWP has no board of directors. Members themselves, in effect, act in this capacity in their monthly meetings, which may draw 20 or 30 people. With over 100 block associations, a corps of 200 to 300 persons provides various services to the organization.

This organization was primarily formed to fight crime. In some other cases, groups started as general-purpose improvement bodies and then moved into crime prevention as their principal concern. This was the case with the Wynnefield Residents' Association in Philadelphia, discussed later in Chapter 3. Whatever the original motivation, viable organizations have resulted.

A number of ways are used to maintain the interest of volunteers in BAWP. A monthly newsletter and occasional bulletins are used to encourage a variety of activities — block parties, summer play streets, barbecues, nightly recreational activities, a food and day care camp, and other projects. "The important thing," Wegener emphasizes, "is to get together. Community activities are the heart of it." In addition, work projects — patrols, workshops, clerical assistance — also help to improve interest and attendance, according to Ross Flanagan.

*Meetings.* But meeting too frequently can burn people out; therefore meetings are designed for relaxation. "You need informality in meetings too if people are to be attracted," emphasizes Ellie Wegener. "Keep it simple. . . .Keep it fun.

Allow time at the end for no business, just getting together, chatting over coffee or punch."

Meetings have influenced the criminal element as well. One burglar changed his ways as he got to know his neighbors better. After he began to attend block association meetings regularly with his wife and got to know members intimately, he could no longer rob people he considered his friends, and he ended up moving out of the neighborhood. Ellie Wegener believes that it is much more difficult for "the criminal to rob people he knows."

The philosophy of the BAWP meetings is positive and preventive, and this climate must be protected. "People who have suffered crime, angry and hurt, tend to poison the community" says Ross Flanagan. "They get people turned against just any black man." BAWP tries to counsel victims, get them to cry, shake it out, he says. "We try to get them before they go out and buy a gun." People frighted or angry often do more damage than good. Flanagan recites the case of a man who shot a boy who had tried to burglarize his house. "This man needs help if he is spraying lead around like that," he stresses.

BAWP has provided the counseling.

*Administration and Design of the Blocks.* Block clubs do not ordinarily operate in a simple square pattern. Under BAWP, a block is the area on both sides of A (see Figure 2-1) but terminated at cross streets B and C at each end of the block.

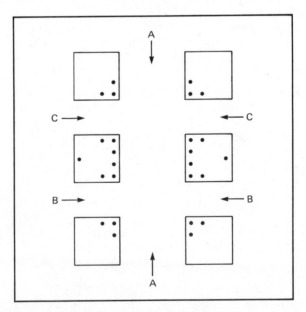

Note: Dots are homes in one block club.

Figure 2-1. Block Club Definition

Everybody in the block is approached for membership in the club. The group will also try to enroll corner homes at border streets B and C and one person from each of the back yard blocks. This provides the club with some control over the bordering streets and blocks.

Clubs are advised to elect two leaders for each block — one from each side of the street — in order to assure that someone is available at all times.

The block chairperson is unpaid. He or she acts as a resource person and is the one to whom fellow block association members first turn in time of crisis. The block leader is expected to solve problems quickly and work out new ideas. He or she must also act as liaison with other blocks and coordinate all relevant activities on the block and in the immediate community. The block chairperson, therefore, is expected to help integrate different clubs — preventing balkanization of the blocks. Great care is taken at all times to promote intra- and inter-block cooperation.

Recordkeeping is exact and crucial in BAWP. The elected secretary should know at all times where a member can be reached in case his or her services are needed in a hurry. Above all, records must show accurate accounts of who is actually on duty patrolling a block at the assigned time. "No shows" cannot be tolerated, say block leaders, because if they are not replaced immediately, neighborhoods go without citizen surveillance during crucial periods.

BAWP provides for setting up new groups. Potential and new members are assured that their privacy will not be invaded. Ample time is provided for the initial sharing of each other's problems, experiences, fears, and solutions. Clubs also realize that they cannot arrive at absolute answers for all problems. They strive to remain flexible enough to meet each contingency as it arises.

**Security Methods.** Besides the regular, daily lookout activities in block association areas, vacation time puts increased demands on the system. Not only do some neighbors watch housing virtually full time, but also the block groups gives explicit instructions to vacationers before they depart. For example, a basic rule is to stop delivery of newspapers during vacation. Nothing is more inviting to a burglar than the accumulation of newspapers on doorsteps; however, stopping delivery is not always successful, as burglars watch for tips such as nondelivery or other bits of information which indicate that families are away from home. In fact, some associations advise residents *not* to cancel subscriptions, but rather to have their neighbors pick up papers every morning and evening.

Other decoy techniques are used too. Residents are urged to install time light switch devices in their homes so that lights go on at dusk and off at dawn. Their neighbors are informed that the mechanism is in operation. If it fails and cannot be readily repaired, a neighbor is instructed to manually turn the lights on and off in the evenings and mornings.

On the street, if a resident suspects that he or she is being followed home, he/she is instructed to ring his/her doorbell before opening the door. This should be done especially when nobody is inside. A person bent on attack is less likely to continue pursuit if it appears that the intended victim has assistance waiting indoors. An alternate approach is also recommended in this situation: go directly to a neighbor's house where someone is likely to be at home.

Other common-sense reminders are constantly communicated to block association members: Do not leave a window open; call the police if you see lights flicker in a house which you believe is empty; call if a stranger is watching your house; call if you see a door open with nobody around. Leaders also report that one should be suspicious when he or she answers the phone and nobody responds. Someone may be checking for a potential burglary.

Some members are advised to place a sign on their front door indicating that they will open doors only for persons whom they expect. Residents are reminded that snowy or rainy days are preferred by burglars because sounds are muted, and people have a tendency to relax their guard during these periods.

In addition, property identification programs are utilized. Personal property is marked with indelible electric pencils, and a sign is put in the door or window indicating that all items are so identified. Thieves generally have more difficulty fencing such goods and are more inclined to pass them by. Secure hardware and impenetrable locks for doors and windows are stressed. Similar methods are promoted in block associations all over the nation.

**How Community Walks Work.** Community walks have been most successful in BAWP. They not only provide block safety but also help to develop a sense of community and neighborhood identity.

Residents volunteer to walk in twos and threes in designated areas during specific times. In addition to their mission to achieve community identity, walks are designed to deter and prevent crime. Simply being on the street contributes to crime prevention. Armed only with freon horns, volunteers stroll the streets watching for anything that looks suspicious. If they observe a crime in progress, they are instructed not to interfere physically. The procedure is to call the police and activate freon horns to alert the neighborhood. Neighbors in turn alert other persons by sounding their own freon horns. Of course, phones are also readily available. Log books are maintained by walkers to record events and to show the addresses of block leaders where immediate assistance can be obtained.

While police may end up chasing the offender, walkers are then free to perform other duties, such as aiding the victim. Providing companionship is important during a period of extreme fright and stress.

Walkers also distribute block association literature and visit aged persons. They watch abandoned houses and the homes of vacationers. Persons wishing to be escorted while grocery shopping or returning home late at night for various reasons are served upon request.

In West Philadelphia's program, each volunteer walks in only one 2-hour shift each month. This relatively infrequent duty assures as little intrusion on a volunteer's time as possible. As a result, volunteers seem to approach their shifts with enthusiasm and freshness.

It is customary to operate two shifts each evening, covering the periods from 7 to 11 o'clock. Each group of two or three volunteers usually covers several blocks. Men, women, and teenagers are encouraged to walk, and dogs may accompany them. As many as ten people are involved in two different area walks each evening. Periods usually marked by higher rates of mischief, such as Halloween and Christmas, require extra shifts. There has been considerable controversy concerning the participation of women. But given the nonviolent approach of community walks, women are active and valuable contributors. They have not requested nor have they received any preferential treatment.

Each walk generally concentrates on one section of the neighborhood. When and where the walk will occur is kept secret, and only those participating are informed of area by the director or coordinator. This is done in order to create maximum impact. An offender may know that walks take place, but he cannot pinpoint where.

*Oakland*

About 900 crime prevention block associations called Home Alert are operating in Oakland. Many began as early as 1966 under guidance of the police department and the Citizen Crime Prevention Committee. Both police and residents praise the program and believe it has had an effect on reducing crime. Predictably, results are most positive where there is good leadership and active participation.

A city of 350,000 people, Oakland has a heavy mixture of minorities: 40 percent of the population is black, 17 percent of Spanish surname (10 percent Chicano), and 5 percent Asian. Block club membership is as heavy for nonwhite as white. There are clubs in black, Spanish, and white neighborhoods. Diverse community leaders helped to kick off the program, but the police department was quick to see its value and reap its benefits. Since then, police officials have been highly supportive and have concentrated on maintaining the visibility of groups and building new ones.

**Activities.** Block association activities here are standard. There are no walking patrols, and mobile activity is limited to Radio Alert which consists of about 3,000 citizen band units in autos which focus on assisting businesses in crime prevention, reporting accidents, and helping in natural disasters. Most recently, Radio Alert also had 90 firms — employing 3,500 drivers with 2,950 radio-equipped vehicles — in the program. At its peak operational phase, Radio Alert had reported more than 200 crimes in progress, 187 automobile accidents, and 152 other incidents requiring police attention. A monthly newsletter has alos helped to keep the program functioning. There is also a Merchant Alert, closely akin to the Home Alert concept, but organized through business associations regardless of location, rather than on an area-by-area basis.

Block associations report crime through regular channels or a hot line set up especially for informants or for those people who do not want to be identified or go through the regular reporting hassle. *Project Identification* — block-by-block stenciling of valuable items by using markers located in all fire houses — and *Operation Roof Top* — painting large home address numbers on several rooftops in each block to assist police helicopters in making quick area identifications — and target hardening of homes are part of the program.

The clubs use house parties and meetings to get to know each other better and to learn about neighborhood issues. The police help with literature, movies, lectures, and some training. Workshops are held on topics other than crime and delinquency to invoke broader interest and participation. The basic plan is to let the criminal know that he or she cannot "rip off" residents in a particular area and get away with it. In some instances, Home Alert leaders have approached troublemakers and directly told them to stay out of the neighborhood. Identifying the criminal and letting him or her know the community is watching has driven many potential troublemakers away.

**Organization.** Home Alert operates in all five of Oakland's police districts and 29 beats but encompasses only about 20,000 people, which means that a majority of blocks are not organized and do not have citizens in the program. A civilian director heads up each district, and he or she coordinates activities with the police district commander. In addition to district heads, there are civilian coordinators who may be responsible for 30 to 36 blocks each and, group leaders are appointed for each block. The police department's goal is to have one coordinator for each beat and a full complement of group leaders for all blocks. The director of a particular district may simultaneously be a beat coordinator and group leader because many times this person is the most interested.

Attendance is mixed, varying from just a few who meet occasionally to regular monthly meetings of 15 to 20 persons. On the other hand, when important issues stir the community, as many as 100 people may gather. Often communication amounts to the group leader's simply contacting interested members whenever possible, distributing literature, and arranging an occasional coffee klatch. Where there are regular meetings, they are informal, usually led by the same persons year after year, and consisting of discussion of issues or techniques or listening to talks by the police and other city officials.

As an example, in the Elmhurst area (24th police district), beat coordinator Robert Rogers makes sure he contacts his members at least one per month, carries on a door-to-door community relations effort, and holds a larger anniversary meeting. He was forced to move three times since 1948, Rogers says, while trying to escape high crime areas. Disrupted enough, he decided to settle down in his well-maintained but little house and make the neighborhood livable. In his sixties, frail, and quiet spoken, Rogers is dedicated to securing a decent living environment for his wife and neighbors. An an experienced older black, it is easier for him to justify to other blacks the importance of caring and improving the quality of life. His crime prevention work takes only a few hours per week, and he sees no reason why he will not continue to stay involved for the rest of his life. The neighbors are happy he is here. One said, "God must have sent you up here with us."

Just a few years ago, Elmhurst was one of the highest crime areas, deteriorating so rapidly that residents asked former Chief of Police Charles R. Gain for extra help. His experienced response was that police can do only so much and that if crime is to be effectively reduced, citizens have got to help themselves. Realizing this was true, a neighborhood minister organized regular meetings, and discussions led to a review of citizen complaints, parking problems, and other matters. But this did not have much effect on crime. However, with police assistance, in a few short months meetings began to center around such things as beat patrol techniques, flexible hours for high crime periods, concentration in the tavern district on drunks and loiterers, changes in zoning to isolate some problems, and promotion of the Home Alert concept. Police presence at meetings improved response, and the dialogue made an excellent impact on both police and residents. According to Chief of Police George Hart, "The whole process worked."

**Home Alert in Public Housing**. Anticrime efforts in Oakland's Public Housing Authority are also effective. Peter Taylor, executive director of the Housing Authority, "got hot on the idea" as the result of serious break-ins and vandalism which made public housing more difficult to manage and "less than a pleasant place to live." One community service aide, Price Holbert, was assigned full-time responsibility for organizing Home Alert among the 15,000 people in more than 4,500 public housing units.

Holbert had to find effective coordinators (equivalent to block leaders) in each building because the job is too big for one person. Most of the people who have volunteered are women between the ages of 19 and 25. There is no budget outside of Holbert's salary, a station wagon, and some folding card tables for meetings. Property identification pens were purchased by the East Oakland Exchange Club and door decals from the Lions Club. Coordinators keep track of the pens and other materials.

Meetings are held in vacant apartments or those of volunteers. The usual police lectures, films, and other services are provided. Volunteers act as "eyes and ears" but do not patrol. Importantly, children are encouraged to attend meetings designed to help both them and the community. Both housing coordinators and regular block club leaders meet periodically to increase motivation and develop common strategies.

Relations with the police are mixed. "Beat sergeants are very cooperative," says Holbert. Principals seem to have few problems; on the other hand, some residents say the police will not cooperate. Police naturally get tired of responding each night to a series of calls in the same building, particularly when they are problems tenants should be able to work out themselves. Some disgruntled residents say the "police can't be bothered with our calls and don't care whether we blow each other's brains out."

Lack of response occurs in many ghetto areas. Importantly, community meetings help to tone down problems and increase understanding; however, as yet not enough residents are interested. "Some are afraid," says Taylor, "afraid of getting ripped off while attending a meeting or fear of reprisal." But in the well-organized buildings, says Holbert, "where I've been able to keep these meetings going it has reduced crime. . . . There are clearly less calls coming in." Holbert says his prime need now is a staff person to help him follow up, arrange meetings, and motivate residents in this huge area.

**Crime Prevention Committee.** Oakland has a Citizens Crime Prevention Committee which has taken the lead to rejuvenate block clubs and enlist the further support of both police and city officials. The main tasks of the committee are to encourage community involvement in the reduction of crime and to maintain crime prevention groups, such as Home Alert, the city's principal volunteer body. Organized in 1966, the committee's twenty-two members were appointed by the mayor, but now the chief of police fulfills this responsibility. The executive committee is composed of two blacks, two whites, two Chicanos, and one Chinese, and the five Home Alert district leaders. The district leaders also head up district subcommittees whose purpose is to promote Home Alert in each area. Two district leaders in particular — Betty Thorson and June Norman — have acted as catalysts to encourage other area leaders to form block clubs and keep them going. The first annual awards dinner (Spring 1975) for block club leaders was arranged by them, and they now intend to make it a yearly affair because of its initial success.

The chairman of the Citizens Crime Prevention Committee, Dr. Kenneth Hoh, a dedicated Home Alert supporter, would like to see the group's responsibilities increased and a modest budget and staff provided. He believes the committee should sit with both police and city officials to help decide citywide police policies and procedures and coordinate the many other organizations involved in crime prevention. Hoh feels greater support for the Home Alert concept is needed from city officials and has outlined proposals for reorganization and promotion, some of which are now being put into effect:

*Organization:*

1. Home Alert needs a formal structure supported by staff and budget;

otherwise, the simple movement of a beat or district leader from an area could cause collapse of many units.

2. Leaders need to be formally trained in depth, and they need to train lower echelons.
3. Each district leader should have a well-trained beat leader as an assistant or second-in-command who could readily replace the top person, if necessary.
4. District leaders need to meet quarterly to discuss problems from a city-wide perspective.
5. Regular workshops for district and beat leaders and other officials should be held to discuss new techniques and policies.

*Promotion:*

1. Focus entire community on Home Alert one full week each year, supported by City Council and the communications media.
2. An award program for volunteers who have contributed the most time and effort.
3. Recognition of service clubs, religious groups, and other organizations which have made substantial contributions to crime prevention.
4. Paid (as well as free) radio and TV time to promote community involvement principles and philosophy.
5. Newsletter prepared by commission staff in cooperation with block groups to convey general items of interest as well as to occasionally feature each Home Alert district.

*Los Angeles*

Los Angeles has a successful community involvement program but a rather loose and flexible block association and block captain concept. The city experienced a 6.6 percent drop in crime in 1973, a rarity among major U.S. municipalities, and Police Chief Edward Davis attributes at least half the decline to community involvement. The city has 3,000 block associations acting as "eyes and ears" for the police department. Residents do not patrol, however, and there is no clamor for active, physical involvement by citizens.

"The police are the public and the public are the police," said Sir Robert Peel, the founder of the modern English police system whom Davis likes to quote. Davis adds, "The police alone cannot prevent crime; in Los Angeles, 600 line officers meet each month with the people."

**Organization.** Community participation in crime suppression exists in several forms in Los Angeles, as block captains, Neighborhood Watch, Neighborhood

Action, Basic Car Plan (BCP) meetings, informal neighborhood meetings or "coffee klatches," or as police support groups, such as the Hollywood Hi-Lites.

Community involvement in Los Angeles is closely tied with the BCP and Team Policing. Under the BCP, which began in 1970, the city's 17 police areas (precincts) were subdivided into 123 basic patrol car districts. Nine patrol officers were assigned to each district for 24-hour protection, and they were required to meet monthly with residents in their district. Crime prevention meetings held in elementary school auditoriums drew from 100 to 300 people. The object was to bring police and the public closer. Part of it was a return to the old "foot-beat cop" who was acquainted personally with the people on his or her beat. This intimacy had been lost when police went into patrol cars and became isolated by glass and steel and the constant 20- to 30-mile-per-hour movement.

The BCP was followed by another Los Angeles Police Department reorganization, Team Policing, in which patrol and traffic officers, detectives, and civilian specialists were merged into single units, each assigned to a "team" territorial division. The team jurisdiction is larger than a BCP district and can take in several of these, but is smaller than an LAPD area (precinct). An area generally includes several teams.

In January 1974, a community involvement program conducive to team policing developed — Neighborhood Action Team Policing (NATP). The more formal neighborhood sessions have given way to informal and more popular gatherings of about 10 or 20 residents in their homes where specific crime and traffic problems are aired. Descriptions of suspects, vehicles, modus operandi hours, and countermeasures are discussed. Alley marking, rooftop numbering, property identification, and watching vacant premises are part of the program. Tips in crime prevention are exchanged, and in some areas monthly newsletters are mailed. Leaders are called block captains, and their names are kept on file at the police department. The police also coordinate home security inspections.

Captain John Konstanturos, head of the LAPD Team Policing Planning Group, said Neighborhood Action (NA) is the primary community involvement program in Los Angeles, and other programs and groups became the means for carrying out and reinforcing NA. Seven of the seventeen police department areas have full team policing with NA, and each of the eleven other areas has at least one team area with NA, according to Lieutenant Frank Isbell, head of the community relations section.

The block program is used most widely in high crime areas, such as the ghettos or South Los Angeles, including Watts. Support groups, particularly women's organizations, dominate the million-population, middle-class suburb of the San Fernando Valley. There the police areas have groups called the Devonshire Dames, the North Hollywood Gals, and the West Valley Blue Bells.

Konstanturos believes that the police department should emphasize a flexible approach, leaving to area commanders the decision as to whether to rely on block captains, one-shot meeting hosts, coffee klatches, or women's support groups. The informal structure and latitude enables police and citizens to shift their focus and meeting place to the problem at hand.

In the high-crime 77th Street Division, Mrs. Estelle Van Meter, who has lived in Watts for the last 15 years and is program coordinator for the 82nd Street Improvement Club, said most of her area has block captains.

One of these captains, Mrs. Viola Collins, said less than half the blocks in her neighborhood are organized, but prospects are good for expanding the program. It is primarily police-sponsored, with no formal organization outside the department.

Sergeant Gary Derks, assistant leader of team 2, said 66 percent of his area has block captains totaling 300, and more are being added. But of the five teams in the Venice area, only a few have block captains. Others rely on neighborhood meetings, coffee klatches, or support groups without captains. Derks says, "The block captain program is a different name for what is essentially the same thing."

**Block Captain Concept.** Not all of the LAPD is sold on the block captain concept. In the Venice experiment with team 28, there were isolated incidents of block captains who were stopped for traffic violations trying to use their identification cards to "badge" themselves out of citations. Further, there were "overzealous" block captains who assumed they were more official members of the department than their status warranted.

Most team members favored coffee klatches over the block captain concept. They felt coffee klatches could be organized and conducted throughout the area without block captains.

Recruiting and administration of the program was time-consuming, requiring one officer in the field full time. A few officers felt that giving citizens a quasi-police status and allowing them to represent the department created problems not worth the benefits.

If the block captain program requires constant recruitment to replace those who move or become disenchanted, then the cost could outweigh the benefits. "It is still much too early, in a one-year test, to predict accurately what kind of a dropout and turnover rate will occur in this type of program."[a]

Captain Konstanturos said the block captain program is a "very expensive, time-consuming process." From a cost standpoint, it is less effective in low crime areas because with fewer offenses to be concerned about, block captains tend to become bored and drop out. More officers are required to maintain an organization. But in high crime areas, police have been able to keep the block captain program going, he says, and it functions as an "outstanding medium of communication."

---

[a]*Final Evaluation of Team 28,* Los Angeles Police Department, April, 1974.

Jay Downer, a city civilian administrative assistant assigned to the Venice area, said some police prefer "block liaison persons" and some prefer coffee klatches with no leaders designated.

From the residents' standpoint, "some don't want to be called block captains because they think they are being called 'snitch' and their house will be blown up. But they will host an informal coffee klatch."

**Police Control and Civilian Patrols.** Block organization is heavily dependent on the police. Samuel Williams, president of the Los Angeles Police Commission, sees no reason to change the system because "police sponsorship ensures the involvement of the police, and that is the basic purpose." He is "unwilling to turn the normal police function over to a private group of citizens," and "questions the value of any program in which unqualified people, who have not undergone stress training, can patrol, stop, and question other people."

One officer, Lieutenant Frank Isbell, is leery of private citizens engaging in active patrol because he believes street contacts can have tragic results. He said that the patrols might attract "frustrated, would-be policemen" who, although well-intentioned, simply might lack the qualifications and/or training for what usually is touchy and sometimes dangerous work.

A similar reaction comes from block captain Mrs. Collins in the 77th Street area: "It's primarily a police function; so, the police should control." She believes that even if groups are independent, the police should censor their activities.

**Comment.** Los Angeles' success in community involvement is due to a good deal of leadership from top police officials which, in turn, has motivated the line officers to accept and actively participate in citizen organization. The idea of letting each area commander experiment and decide which approach is best for her or his area has worked well. The prevalent feeling seems to be that it does not make much difference whether it is the concept of block captains or any other effective means of getting people to meet and watch their neighborhoods that is used. The essential idea of motivating residents and increasing the understanding between police and citizens appears to be most important. On the other hand, there are thousands of block associations and block captains who provide the substance and means for success in achieving these goals.

*Compton*

Compton is a different experience from the two larger cities already discussed. Its crime rate is dramatically high. It has a 95 percent minority population, and block clubs are as loosely organized here as in largely white communities. Being in the middle-range size of cities, Compton offers a valuable experience to cities of its size and smaller. However, total city population size has little effect on the performance of block associations which depend primarily on the activities of each block club.

**Local Conditions.** Adjacent to Los Angeles' Watts, Compton has 80,000 people and many of the same crime problems which have besieged Watts. Gang fights among juveniles, assaults, muggings, and shakedowns have not been uncommon.

The city is between 75 and 80 percent black, 15 to 20 percent Mexican-American, and about 5 percent white. With a median age of only 19.7, it has one of the nation's youngest populations. In a real sense, youth, at least a part of it, has been Compton's biggest problem. The city's new and energetic Police Chief, Thomas Cochee, succinctly described the situation as one involving about 200 offenders, nearly all juveniles, who commit about 75 percent of Compton's crimes.

It would be a gross understatement to conclude that Compton's economic trends have been unkind to its youth. While the city's overall unemployment rate was a startling 11 percent in early 1974, over half its young people had no jobs, with most also unemployable and lacking job skill training. Needless to say, their financial future does not look bright in Compton. In the city as a whole, 35 percent of the residents receive some kind of welfare assistance. As for housing, out of 24,000 structures, 1,700 are vacant. One might agree that these conditions are ripe for crime.

**Activities and Objectives.** Compton makes use of both mobile patrols and block clubs. And the police department operates related crime prevention programs, such as Citizen Ride-Along, Foot Patrol, Police Athletic League, Juvenile Anti-Gang Detail, Law Enforcement Explorer Scout Program, and Reserve Officer Corps.

Despite the city's serious problems, Chief Cochee has formulated some worthy objectives. These include reducing burglary by 10 percent over the previous year's figure, reducing traffic accidents by 10 percent, reducing response time, increasing average patrol time 15 percent per watch, increasing training classes 25 percent, decreasing personnel complaints 25 percent, increasing reserve corps strength by 25 percent, and increasing community involvement in crime prevention activities by 50 percent.

Community involvement through the use of block clubs has become a major objective. "The community will be experiencing a tremendous effort to organize blocks of residents into viable groups to combat burglaries," said Chief Cochee. And Sergeant Arthur Camarillo, crime prevention project coordinator, hopes to have block clubs in every major section of the city. He increased the number of clubs from 9 in early 1974 to 31 by the year's end. And he hopes to create from three to five more per month. Further, a community-based coalition of block clubs and civic groups has formed Block Central to coordinate and maintain the program.

A police department report on block clubs states:

In the areas where people have organized block clubs and have instituted the neighborhood watch program, there has been a significant reduction in burglaries and in most areas, an elimination of burglaries and other felonious crimes. The results have been tremendous in assisting organizational efforts for the program.[b]

At the latest count, over 40 block clubs have been formed, and the city's efforts are proceeding strongly in this direction.

*New York*

The Block Security Program (BSP) in New York City is a unique concept. It was established by former Mayor John Lindsay as part of the Police Department's Crime Prevention Unit, in April 1973. A Block Security Guidelines Board develops policies, and the city's Office of Neighborhood Affairs (formerly Office of Neighborhood Government) oversees the administration of funds which are used to match block association contributions. In the first year, $7 million of city money was provided, and in the second, under Mayor Abraham Beame's administration, another $5 million was allocated. The police department is enthusiastic about the program, and participating residents feel confident that it does help reduce crime and fear.

**Purpose.** The matching fund program has helped greatly to activate groups, but usually some serious problem motivated most groups to get started, according to Sergeant Joseph Mannino. Public response has been positive from the black and white population and from high- and low-income groups. Participants are mostly middle-aged, 40 to 50 years old, and besides crime they are concerned with general neighborhood improvement. The city distributes literature which stresses a better environment and a new system of neighborhood government.

**Matching Funds.** Each police precinct receives a minimum of $20,000 for matching purposes annually and additional amounts based on population. Groups can receive a maximum of $10,000 each on a matching basis. The city will match an association as follows: $9 to every $1 the association raises up to a total of $500 ($450 city, $50 association); $4 to $1 for the next $5,000; $2 to $1 for anything from $4,400 to $10,000. This means that an association can acquire $10,000 for an investment of $3,825.

---

[b]*Block Clubs,* Compton Police Department Report, 1974.

Expenditures are limited to hardware items, such as outdoor lighting, burglar alarms, closed-circuit television, solid-core or steel doors, deadbolt or dropbolt locks, window bars or screens, intercoms, walkie-talkies, mobile radios, fencing, mirrors, and property identification tools. Funds cannot be used for overhead, personnel, printing, weapons, watchdogs, barbed wire, automobiles or their maintenance, and private residence under three units. Groups can come back each year for additional money.

The precinct commanding officer approves groups for funds, and the precinct crime prevention officer conducts the basic investigations. The Crime Prevention Unit at headquarters follows up and monitors the whole operation. Besides emphasis on target hardening, the "eyes and ears" aspect is a critical part of the program; so is developing a "god neighborhood" attitude of looking out for each other. Members are trained to know everyone who lives in their block or building and to keep an eye on the backs of buildings or other more secluded spots. "If no one cares about your door," says Lieutenant Henry A. Ludwicki, who manages this crime prevention program, "and that burglar is aware of that — he can spend the whole damn day at that door. He can blow it up with dynamite if no one's going to call us. This is why policemen want block associations."

**Eligibility for Receiving Funds.** A variety of associations can receive funds. These include block and neighborhood groups, tenant associations in apartment buildings, merchant groups, and volunteer mobile and foot patrols. To be eligible, merchant groups must include at least 24 businesses at street levels or one flight up with entrances leading directly onto the street. Block associations must represent at least 35 households and must have at least 35 members over 18 years of age. Care is taken not to fund the wrong kind of group. "We must safeguard against vigilantes," says Lieutenant Ludwicki. "In approving funds we make sure that this is not a vigilante group coming up."

Geographical contiguity is required. The minimum area for a block association is both sides of one city block. Tenant groups can represent one or more apartment buildings, and only one association can be funded in each building. However, resident and merchant associations can geographically overlap. "Special-purpose" organizations — such as mobile patrols — can also be funded for the same area as a resident group as long as there is no functional duplication.

Each association must have a written set of bylaws, collect dues, hold meetings on a regular basis (at least once a month), and have a minimum of three elected officers. One of its members must be designated Block Security Officer and must not be an employee of the police department. He or she is liaison with the police and must successfully complete a training program, which consists of about 8 hours of instruction on locks and other hardware and general security problems. The Block Security Officer is required to develop a Block Security Plan and budget for his or her area.

By October 1974, 667 applications for funding were approved, but only

151 had received funds or purchased equipment. Of the total number of block associations seeking funds, 28 percent were formed expressly as a response to the crime problem, according to Captain Richard J. Condon, commander of the Crime Prevention Section.

**Federations of Block Associations.** Block associations tend to band together in federations in order to develop more viable organizations and to mutually assist each other. The federations help block clubs to develop crime prevention plans and to receive city funds. Examples of some federations in New York City are the United Block Associations, Manhattan (East Harlem), United Block Association of Hyde Park (Brooklyn), Yorkville Alliance of Block Associations (Manhattan), Bushwick Block Captains Association (Brooklyn), Bay Ridge Council of Block Associations (Brooklyn), Tottenville Improvement Council (Staten Island), and Federation of West Side Block Associations (Manhattan). The West Side Association is considered one of the most effective. It has 45 member groups under its umbrella, each with about 1,000 families in a total area of 290,000 people. As many as 3,000 persons reside in a block in this area compared to approximately 1,500 in typical blocks in Brooklyn, for example. West Side's annual budget is about $4,000 and comes from dues of $10 from each group, from block parties and plant sales, and other promotional activities.

The federations are nonpartisan entities but exert strong pressures on government to get things done. Meeting agenda have expanded over the years to include such things as better city services, consumer affairs, ecology, zoning, development of malls, beautification, and other things. An analysis of certain aspects of police performance by the West Side group, for example, resulted in the transfer of 90 officers (out of 273) to other precincts. "Residents now enjoy excellent communication with police officials, police response time has improved considerably, and generally residents are more at ease," says Edward Schwarzer, West Side's chairman and founder. He is now engaged in an effort to coordinate block groups citywide under a plan called *Neighborhoods in Action.*

# 3

Mobile Patrols

## Organizing Mobile Units

### *Starting Mobile Patrols*

Block clubs usually do not constitute a large enough area by themselves to be able to organize and operate community walks or mobile patrols. A federation of block clubs or other areawide organization is the most frequently used method to organize and oversee mobile patrols. Existing neighborhood-improvement organizations can also be used for this purpose. Civilian radio patrols, taxi and trucking companies, and other operating concerns are usually already in a good position to set up mobile crime prevention units if they so desire.

Patrols may be established by any private or public group interested and sufficiently responsive to do a good job. Separate patrols may be established citywide by any or all the above organizations as long as central coordination, supervision, and rules and regulations are provided by the police department.

**Patrol Areas.** Block Clubs and watchers can be set up on almost any block; however, mobile patrols are much more complex and work better in certain areas. In some of the highest crime districts, it may be too dangerous for unarmed civilians to patrol in cars or on foot. This may be particularly true where organized youth gangs exist or where there has been a series of stabbings or beatings. On the other hand, under proper police protection and response, civilian patrols have proved highly effective in some cities even in the most serious crime districts.

The regular travels of taxis, trucks, city vehicles, and cars with amateur radios bring them in contact with all areas of the city. In some cases, off-duty private and public drivers have been organized to patrol specific areas during critical hours. Amateur radio patrols seem to have an enduring quality because of the interest of members in radio communication and the opportunity to learn more about a subject in which they are very much interested.

**Police Role.** Mobile patrols can be effective in most city neighborhoods, around shopping areas, and in specially selected districts where police need and welcome this kind of assitance. Mobile patrols can make police more responsive but usually only if they work hand in hand with the police department so that each

33

knows what the other is doing. Police officials should endorse the program, yet in some cases, civilians may start and successfully operate their own patrols without police approval, if this is warranted and the only way it can be done under local conditions. In any case, patrols must not be vigilantes. The police department should be prepared to stop such groups immediately. This will prevent any widespread deterioration and demonstrate the correct direction for other groups wishing to organize.

**Objectives.** The objectives of mobile groups vary, but are similar to those of block clubs. They are primarily concerned with the field of crime prevention, but some engage in almost anything that affects the neighborhood, from stopping the opening of undesirable establishments to lobbying high-level officials for more police protection. As an example, the specific objectives of one group are as follows: (1) to establish a continuing system of volunteer civilian patrols as a deterrent to crime, (2) to help prevent juvenile delinquency, (3) to help organize block groups which will take care of security precautions needed on a block-by-block basis, (4) to alert individuals to security measures which should be taken by every resident, and (5) to alert people to the availability of federal theft insurance.

*Organization*

When organizing a mobile patrol, the following elements should be considered:

1. *Basic requirements.* Patrol members should be at least 18 years of age, be issued identification cards, and possess an FCC license wherever radios are used. Although males predominate, many women patrol too, and teams are racially integrated in mixed ethnic areas.

   The method of identifying patrol members should be determined by the police area commander. Some departments require automobile identification insignia and jackets or clearly visible patches for members. In some cases, visible identification could lessen the effectiveness of the patrol's function. Under any circumstances, descriptions of the automobiles in the patrol, hours of operation, and other vital information of the patrol participants should be given to the police department.

2. *Equipment.* Patrol members use their own vehicles. If resources are available, patrol vehicles could be equipped with cameras, fire extinguishers, oxygen, gas masks, tools, and other life-saving items. The most important piece of equipment is the two-way radio, although patrol members can be effective by simply observing and using the public telephone system.

3. *Work hours.* Long working shifts should not be required of volunteers.

Usually 4-hour shifts once or twice monthly are sufficiently demanding. Patrols normally operate during the highest crime periods.

4. *Don'ts.* There are a number of don'ts: no weapons, no sirens, no special emergency lights, no physical contact, no automobile chases, no detaining anyone, no questioning, and no response to police transmissions. Of course, civilian radio bands must be used properly. The organization should do its own monitoring of abuses by fines, dismissals, or whatever action is most appropriate. In some jurisdictions, patrol members carry weapons and engage in active pursuit. We prefer the eyes-and-ears functions and assistance to victims of crime. In any case, the police department should issue rules and regulations, monitor civilian operations, and discipline groups.

5. *Budget.* Volunteers vitally interested in their neighborhood will normally not require compensation. Most of the time civic responsibility is the best approach; however, where possible, gasoline and some minor expenses ought to be paid. Some organizers may have to be paid on a part-time basis in order to keep the project going over a long period of time. Matching fund programs and other sources of funds should be considered if long-term viability is expected.

6. *Keeping records.* In general volunteers will not maintain elaborate records. Reporting forms and detailed records should not be expected of private patrols. Useful descriptons and reporting of major incidents and follow-up information should be the primary requirements.

7. *Nonformality.* Except for very formal operations, rank, uniforms, and stringent rules are to be avoided in order to hold the interest of the average volunteer. Those wishing greater formality normally pursue such programs as the auxiliary police, community service officer, or other closely supervised police functions. However, some mobile patrols do follow regular police ranks — major, captain, lieutenant, sergeant, and officer — and designate them on their uniforms.

8. Obviously more formal programs, closely linked to the police department, require careful screening of recruits. Fingerprints, criminal and traffic records, medical history, drug and alcohol use, and educational level should be investigated.

9. Training patrol members is highly desirable and instills greater trust and loyalty in the organization. The police academy usually provides assistance for training. Areas to be covered should include at least the following:

   *a.* Fundamental law and basic city ordinances

   *b.* What constitutes crime and situations worthy of calling for police assistance

   *c.* First-aid and emergency care

   *d.* Auto safety and general vehicle maintenance.

   *e.* Proper radio language and usage

   *f.* Common-sense street psychology received by regular police officers


*Activities*

1. *Eyes and ears.* The eyes and ears function is the main activity. Some patrols are encouraged to follow offenders as long as they are not in "hot pursuit."

2. *Lights and horns.* Headlights, horns, flashlights, and searchlights should be used to spot and chase away offenders. Cameras should be carried and pictures taken of offenders. In emergencies, patrols should continuously sound their automobile horns and direct headlights and flashlights at offenders. This frightens criminals, alerts the police, and warns neighbors. Residents should be instructed to call police when they hear this signal. During this period patrol members should not get out of their cars. Volunteers are instructed not to carry weapons and to avoid physical confrontations. Their role is to frighten off offenders and summon police officers. Where a club base station exists, calls are relayed to police.

3. *Dogs.* Dogs are also encouraged to discourage the potential criminal, even if only household pets are used. The offender is not inclined to find out what purpose the dog serves. One trained dog can be a deterrent well beyond his actual availability. The association believes that once the word is out that such an animal is being used, a member's own pet can cause concern to a potential offender. The criminal cannot be certain whether the dog in the patrol car is the trained attack dog or not.

4. *Watching property.* Until police arrive members should be instructed to watch homes which have been broken into. Of course, vacant property and homes of vacationers should be on the patrol list for observance. Ideally police will cooperate and provide such listings to responsible groups.

5. *Patrol locations.* Members should change their patrol habits regularly as well as concentrating on the higher crime areas. Obviously to preserve the element of uncertainty and surprise, patrol schedules should not be publicized. Arrangements should be made to patrol shopping centers, parking lots, bus stops, schools, and other frequented spots. Announcements have proved effective in deterring crime; therefore, posters and other communication media should be used to inform as many people as possible that the neighborhood is under block association protection.

## Case Histories of Mobile Operations

Case histories of some important and instructive mobile patrols will provide valuable lessons for setting up units in almost any city. Let us discuss a variety of models.

### Secure All Wynnefield In Philadelphia

The mobile patrol in Wynnefield, a section of Philadelphia, is a typical operation. Geographically, the 150 blocks of Wynnefield contain mostly Tudor-style row houses occupied primarily by middle-class blacks and older middle-class Jewish residents. About 65 percent of the population is black and 35 percent white.

The program started after a series of stabbings in the neighborhood, each committed against an elderly white woman — a stab in the back and a quick escape. Charles Bowser, executive director of Philadelphia's Urban Coalitiion, became aroused and motivated for action. Eventually he formed a group called Secure East Wynnefield. By the second meeting at Har Zion Synagogue, large numbers of people attended from many areas. They expressed impatience with crime and a desire for a communitywide organization. So the group was expanded and the name changed to Secure All Wynnefield (SAW).

**Objectives.** The objective of the group is primarily crime prevention, but it engages in almost anything that affects the neighborhood, from stopping the opening of undesirable establishments to lobbying high-level officials for more police protection. More specifically, the objectives are as follows: (1) to establish a continuing system of volunteer civilian patrols as a deterrent to crime, (2) to help prevent juvenile delinquency, (3) to help organize block groups which will take care of security precautions needed on a block-by-block basis, (4) to alert individuals to security measures which should be taken by every Wynnefield resident, and (5) to alert people to the availability of federal theft insurance.

**Organization.** Prior to this, another neighborhood improvement group, Wynnefield Residents' Association, functioned here under Executive Director Sharon Glaser. With the new interest in crime prevention, the two groups decided to merge, and Glaser became the director of the new group. At first, volunteer support grew rapidly but then fell off when one of the alleged killers in the neighborhood, the son of a black minister, was arrested and brought to trial. Although he had confessed, he was acquitted. A second trial for the same person — but for another crime — resulted in a hung jury. Meanwhile interest was high, but shortly, in about five months, work pressure on the all volunteer staff became too great and their time too limited. Moreover, they were unable to replace themselves with new volunteers.

SAW was in trouble, but fortunately it got new life through federal funding and some private money. A grant of $22,700 from LEAA, $1,500 donated by the Philadelphia Regional Jewish Community Relations Council, $1,500 raised by SAW, and $3,527 from Wynnefield Residents Association have been the source of salaries for the three staff and overhead costs. Besides the director, a community worker oversees the block clubs and patrols, and a youth worker recruits and supervises volunteers who, in turn, work with about 300 youths. The funds are keeping 138 volunteers riding patrols, 20 in the contact squad to remind patrol members of schedules, 10 in marking, 30 in a Wynnefield youth recreation program, and 8 volunteer teachers who give GED high school assistance. In addition, each of the clubs has its own block leader and helpers. According to Glaser, in any one block there is a core of 15 to 20 people out of about 80 who are very active; there are also approximately the same number who never participate. About another 40 or 50 people float in and out depending on the issue under consideration.

The association's mood is businesslike and less missionary than BAWP's, for example. However, there is the usual problem of trying to keep volunteers. They tend to "run out of steam after a time," says Sharon Glaser. "You've got to remember that they must get something out of it. . . . If you remind them, they are more willing to serve." Someone has to do this regularly. "If you do not have staff," she says, "you lose continuity."

SAW has the advantage of having joined the ongoing 15-year-old Wynnefield Residents' Association, which regularly communicates with 4,000 of the 5,500 households in the area and has maintained 700 dues-paying families. SAW has at least one member on 130 of the 150 blocks in Wynnefield and 58 organized block clubs, largely put together by the Wynnefield Association. SAW has its own 30-member steering council and is autonomous from the Wynnefield Residents' Association, but board members from each group sit on both boards, and their purposes are closely related.

**Method of Operation.** Mobile patrols are the basic mechanism for street security by volunteers in Wynnefield, and more than 100 members of the Wynnefield Residents' Association participate regularly. They drive their own cars and work on 3-hour shifts with two persons per car. Each volunteer is asked to serve one shift each month, but some serve more often. Although men predominate, women serve too, and all teams are racially integrated and nonvigilante. Patrols operate every night during the highest crime period — 7 P.M. to 1 A.M. There are few daytime patrols.

Patrols report suspicious events to the police by walkie-talkies and pay phones. In extreme emergencies they continuously sound their automobile horns and direct headlights and flashlights at offenders. This frightens criminals, alerts the police, and warns neighbors. Residents are also urged to call police when they hear this signal. Volunteers are taught not to get out of their cars. They carry no weapons and are instructed to avoid any physical confrontations. Their role is to frighten off offenders and summon police officers. An association base station receives calls and relays them to the police.

An innovation for SAW is now being considered. At least one trained attack dog is planned for the patrols. As one association leader observed, "With dogs you don't have to depend on the police getting there in time to catch the man. You can get the dog to get hold of that person and keep him there until the police arrive." One trained dog can be a deterrent well beyond his or her actual availability. The association believes that once the word is out that such an animal is being used, a member's own pet can cause concern to a potential offender. The criminal could not be certain whether the dog in the patrol car is the trained attack dog or not.

Patrol schedules are not publicized, obviously to preserve the element of uncertainty and surprise. Importantly, posters indicate that the neighborhood is under association protection. These announcements, in conjunction with the patrols themselves, have proved effective.

Both residents and police believe that crime has decreased in Wynnefield. Recently, few patrols have encountered crimes in progress. Wynnefield residents are justly proud of this and hope and expect that crime will continue to remain lower in their area.

**Wynnefield Block Clubs**. The regular block clubs in Wynnefield have been effective too and keep in close contact with the mobile patrols. Many families who do not care to participate in patrols do join the block clubs. Estelle Cooper, an older black woman, says she has 18 households out of 55 in her club. Although only four members are men, other males pitch in on special projects when asked. Most participants are middle-aged, married, and homeowners.

Ms. Cooper says, "You can do a lot by just watching. We report teenage gangs on the corners and watch houses reported to be dealing in drugs." She says that an increase in drug traffic is easy to spot.

Although Ms. Cooper receives a lot of calls from her neighbors about potential problems, she does not seem to mind. "People on the block are more aware of what's happening and that's good." She scoffs that some of the comments that she represents a "bunch of gossiping old ladies." Ms. Cooper is respected by the neighborhood as a whole and by city officials, and is a grandmother image to the area's children. Having left a neighborhood overrun with gangs and killing, she decided to stick it out here.

*Our Neighbors Civic Association — Philadelphia*

Another group is Philadelphia which has made use of mobile patrols is Our Neighbors Civic Association. However, it has run into difficulty because of trying to mix programs of different purposes and because of extreme crime and social characteristics in the area. It offers valuable lessons and is worth describing here, at least briefly.

The program operates in an area where 98 percent of the population is black and in one of the highest crime districts, with several active youth gangs and large-scale housing deterioration. Reducing crime is not so easy here, not just because it has already reached such high proportions but because there is less interest in doing anything about it, less hope, more fear, and fewer leaders. Yet some people who make this area their home are doing something about it.

**Origins and Purpose.** In 1968, following the nation's urban riots, the Urban Coalition in Philadelphia agreed to fund Our Neighbors Civic Association on the basis of a proposal written by several young members. This initial funding was for youth activities involving gang types under 25 years of age. But the program did not materially alleviate community problems and, furthermore, got out of control by straying from its objectives. In short, "it did not work out," and it was dropped in its initial form.

In 1970, youth gang wars broke out in the area. In particular, two gangs, the Morocco's and Demarco's, clashed and one youth was killed. As a result of this crisis, Bertha Brown, director of the neighborhood association, called the radio and press media to exhort the community's dilemma and provoke citizens into action. Local meetings were called, and groups such as the Black Panthers, youth organizations, religious bodies, and others attended.

In 1971, a program was finally agreed on that the Urban Coalition could fund. It revolved around law enforcement and was the first community patrol in the city to be funded by the Urban Coalition. Previous programs were limited to unpaid volunteers.

The program operated out of the Civic Association's four-room corner storefront and immediately ran into trouble from those who saw it as a threat to their domination of the neighborhood. The center was robbed six times. Six walkie-talkies and the main transmitter were stolen. In response to this misfortune, the Urban Coalition purchased more equipment but of a poorer quality. Bars and screens were placed on the windows. The center linked up with the Radio Alert Patrol, but intense problems continued to keep the law enforcement part of this program from success. In early 1974, the energy crisis caused gasoline shortages so intense that volunteers, who were using their private cars for patrol, simply stopped driving.

However, a new budget calls for gas for volunteers, a full-time coordinator to recruit and supervise volunteers, radios and transmitters, and other necessities. The program now has three major responsibilities: (1) mobile patrols; (2) mothers walking around schools and in main corridors; and (3) "eyes and ears" for reporting crime. This is a big change from the project's normal preventive activities which have involved some 200 participants in such things as cultural and recreation programs, teenage girls clubs, homework center, family counseling, and information and referral.

**The Future.** It is possible that concentrating on crime prevention could damage the social programs and yet not be sufficiently effective for law enforcement. Ms. Brown is neither enthusiastic nor optimistic about the law enforcement part. She understands the necessity for creating a safer neighborhood, and over the years has worked toward this. However, cutting back on social programming would hurt. Youth gangs are not threatened by social and recreation programs, but they are apprehensive about community safety patrols. They would not be averse to destroying both rather than be threatened by either, according to local residents. In more peaceful neighborhoods the two might fit together, but here it is questionable. A better solution would appear to be a separate program in a different physical setting and with new leadership.

**Walking Patrols.** Not much is done here in the way of walking patrols. In one area, near a junior high school, a squad of fifteen men prefer to walk and "rap" with juveniles "to put them on notice" and to develop friendships; confrontation is avoided. Several block clubs in the Wynnefield area tried walking patrols but dropped the idea. "With a car you don't lose people because of the cold in winter or the heat in summer," says Sharon Glaser of the SAW group. Here, too, residents have been afraid to walk the neighborhood because of the irrational series of back stabbings that occurred prior to the mobile patrols. On the other hand, Mrs. Glaser says, "If I were starting now, I would give a lot of thought to it [setting up walks]."

*Mobile Patrols: Chicago*

Chicago now has two successful Citizen Radio Patrol programs, but this has not always been the case. The city's first citizen patrol was formed on the South Side in the late 1960s. It received widespread coverage in local newspapers because of its vigilante-type approach. The police, aware of the problems such activities would create, adopted a stay-clear policy toward any citizen organization of this nature. The lack of police cooperation caused residents to forego the idea of armed patrols and to develop other means of protecting their neighborhoods. The concept of mobile patrols was retained.

    In time, police support for unarmed citizen groups patrolling their own neighborhoods grew. On April 30, 1973, at a time when more than thirty patrols were operating throughout the city, the police department sponsored a meeting to do two things: "(1) provide a catalyst to bring the groups together to share information, and (2) provide the department with a vehicle for monitoring patrol personnel and activities." At the second citywide meeting, the department presented a list of thirty proposed rules and regulations of conduct for citizen radio patrol organizations. Ten of these were accepted by members present and govern the current activities of the patrols.

### Mobile Patrol Rules and Regulations

1. Units must carry issued Chicago Police Department Identification cards at all times while on duty.
2. No firearms are authorized while in the performance of assigned duties.
3. No member will leave his or her automobile to investigate any suspicious activity.
4. Members will assist a police officer only upon the officer's specific request.
5. No member will represent himself/herself as a police officer to anyone under any conditions.
6. No member will participate in an automobile chase under any circumstances.
7. No member will detain anyone unless ordered to do so by a police officer.
8. No member is authorized to question anyone.
9. No member with a Chicago Police Department Monitor may respond to Chicago Police Department transmissions.
10. Patrolling members must be at least 18 years of age. (Age requirements are waived for all other functions of the organization.)

There are no exceptions to the above rules and regulations. Any member violating any of these is automatically removed from the organization. In only one instance, involving an illegal arrest, a member had to be dismissed by the group for a violation. Also, all members must acquire FCC licenses and abide by their rules as well. In one case, a member was dismissed for violating FCC regulations and making "the patrol look bad by using vulgar language on the radio."

The Chicago Police Department has specific rules regarding civilian patrols for police officers too. No off-duty officers are allowed to participate in civilian patrols. This is primarily because department policy requires them to be armed at all times, which could endanger civilian partners. Nevertheless, it is believed that some officers participate despite this policy, but usually patrol alone.

Today, thirty-one patrols operate throughout the city using these rules and regulations and with the full support of Chicago police officers.

Because of a growing interest in crime prevention in predominantly black communities, a majority of the patrols are black.

**The Lakeview Radio Patrol.** The Lakeview community lies on Chicago's mid-North Side, stretching from the shore of Lake Michigan west to the Chicago

River and from Fullerton Avenue north to Montrose Avenue. It encompasses the entire 19th (Town Hall) police district.

Lakeview's population is a microcosm of the entire city. It spans the gamut from the super-rich along famed Lake Shore Drive to the low-income families residing in Lathrop Homes, a public housing project. Young professionals fill high-rises and brownstones surrounding New Town, an area of bars, boutiques, and brothels. Lower-middle-income whites, Latins, and some blacks share the remainder of the area, living in small single-family homes and rented apartments. The growth in New Town's population and the advent of teenage gang activities here have resulted in a serious increase in crime over the past decade.

In February, 1973, a young ham radio operator was driving home when he spotted a building on fire. He tuned his citizen band radio on the nationwide emergency frequency in an attempt to call for help but could not reach anybody. Tuning immediately to the frequency which he and his ham radio friends usually used, he contacted his wife who was monitoring the radio at home, and she called the fire department.

Subsequently, a group of sixteen citizen band radio operators protested the ineffectiveness of the nationally recognized emergency network. Thus, the Lakeview Radio Patrol was born out of a mutual interest in radio communication and concern for the safety of their neighborhood. The group is now a not-for-profit, state-chartered corporation with a board of directors and officers and its own set of by-laws. Although all members are part-time volunteers, a number of them insist that patrols "take up 90 percent of their nonworking time."

**Chatham Park Manor Patrol.** To a large extent, the success of the Chatham Park Manor Patrol depends on the personality of its chairman, Isaac H. Hawkins, Jr. "He's terrific, a marvel. Isaac is one of those guys you're always astounded at. He's always at it, and there's absolutely nothing in it for him," police officials say.

The group decided that their original name, Citizen's Enforcement Patrol, was intimidating and implied, incorrectly, that they used vigilante tactics, so the name was changed to Chatham Park Manor Patrol, and membership grew. Unlike the Lakeview group, none of the members had an interest in citizen band radios prior to formation. Their base radio was donated at a community meeting by 6th Ward Alderman, Eugene Sawyer. Volunteers purchased their own transmitters, and another group, the successful South Shore Patrol, trained them in use of the equipment.

Originally, members were assessed in order to raise operating funds. For the past two years, the patrol has received a percentage of money from the Chatham-Avalon Park Community Council's annual fund raising Las Vegas night. Other block clubs and individuals donate also. The money has been used for office supplies, gas stipends, equipment maintenance, and the purpose of six radio transmitters.

Currently, there are 37 radio patrol volunteers, 25 of whom are active. The active members are black, and two are women. The part-time helpers are white, blue-collar workers or retirees. The average age is 50 years. The patrols operate 5 days per week with from 1 to 16 units on duty at any one time, depending on the level of projected criminal activity.

There is little doubt that the Chatham Park Manor Patrol is effective. Any police officer involved with the operation will verify that the very presence of the mobile units in the street is having some effect on the deterrence of crime in the area. It is also having a psychological effect on the community. Local shop-keepers are beginning to stay open after dark, and residents feel safer walking the streets.

The activities of the mobile patrol, however, seem to take second place to Isaac Hawkins' not-so-hidden "hidden agenda." Hawkins, concerned citizen and employee of the Chicago Post Office, is attempting to organize the entire city into a vast radio patrol.

He is far from pleased with his success to date. Still, he remains optimistic and takes a philosophical approach to the problems, viewing citizen apathy as one of the reasons for continued fear and loss of personal freedom. People want to use their time to do "their own thing," and for most of them, "crime preven-tion is not their thing," he says.

The apathy encountered does not seem to discourage Hawkins inordinately. Residents who do participate in the patrol's four-point program seem to do so with enthuasism. Membership in the mobile unit is stable, and the operation runs smoothly.

He believes, however, that he must secure the support and cooperation of the city administration before he can attract new volunteers to the patrol and expand activities to other areas of the city. To this end, he keeps in constant contact with key officials. He has identified a potential funding source in the Illinois Law Enforcement Commission — the state planning agency for U.S. Department of Justice funding. He is now pressing the police to apply for funds to establish a centrally located, citywide citizen band radio network with fre-quency set aside for Citizen Radio Patrols. But the police department approaches coapplicant contract programs with citizens groups with great hesi-tation. Accountability is the main concern.

Hawkins is not finding a great deal of desire for federal funds even from among Citizen Radio Patrols. The fear of outside funding implies outside con-trol, and many of the patrols want no part of this. Opponents point to the un-fortunate experience of the one local patrol that did receive short-term LEAA funds. A paid staff was employed to organize operations. The volunteers, who continued to pay for upkeep of their equipment and to buy their own gas, be-came disillusioned and dropped out of the patrol. When funding ran out, the level of participation returned to normal. But even this experience does not de-ter Isaac Hawkins from his quest. He says that he would use funds in a different manner and that his program has little relationship to other experiences.

**Citywide Citizen Radio Patrol.** At the citywide level, the Citizen Radio Patrol is an excellent volunteer resource. Meetings are held at police headquarters every three or four months. Police officers who attend say, "They [meetings] are a good indication of how the citizenry is beginning to use its own resources — time gas, equipment — to respond to police problems." Such is the belief of Lieutenant Paul Blaney, Commander of the Business and Youth Crime Prevention Section of the Community Service Bureau of the Chicago Police Department, and also designated liaison to the Citizen Radio Patrols. Lieutenant Robert E. McCann, in charge of the Community Service Bureau, stated, "It's terrific when police officers go to meetings with people like that."

The meetings can be of benefit far beyond a mere exchange of information. Some patrols have lost members because the job is "basically thankless." The meetings can and have served as a forum to announce the oustanding achievements of individual members and patrols. The distribution of official crime report forms, designed especially for use by Citizen Radio Patrols, was in itself a recognition of the value and legitimacy of the work being done. Strangely enough, although members seem pleased to receive these forms — accepting them as a token of recognition — they are rarely returned to headquarters as requested. This is true despite arrangements made to forward them through the districts by way of stamped, self-addressed envelopes provided by the police.

It is believed that some of the patrols actively avoid recognition and publicity out of fear of reprisal. In some communities, there have been incidents of tire slashings and sniper attacks.

Meetings have not yet been used as training sessions. Currently, any training done by headquarters personnel is done upon request through the local patrol meetings. In one case, a Spanish-speaking group wanted to start a patrol in their area. They had no car and no radio at their disposal when they began to organize. Before they tackled those problems, however, the leadership wanted to ensure that potential volunteers were adequately trained. A Latino officer was assigned to work with them for about 6 months. Once they were trained, they obtained the needed equipment and ever since have been successfully patrolling their community.

The police seem ambivalent in regard to any more formalized training for patrol members. They did, however, seem interested in the suggestion that the local community college system offer classes in such areas as patrol patterns, communication techniques, and law for college credit through its adult education program. The colleges already offer courses for Chicago police recruits, youth officers, communication dispatchers, and other in-service officers. Furthermore, patrol members like the education idea.

Based on the nearly two years of close cooperation with the patrols, Chicago police officials seem highly pleased with their effort. They see the primary reason for success as the noninterference on the part of the patrols in police business. According to police officials, "Citizen comments on police administrative matters can destroy police-community relations. They simply do not understand the problems. Criticism of individual policemen on a personal level can be harmful, and citizens playing cops and robbers present an intolerable situation." Radio patrols have not interfered.

Ultimately, the rules and regulations set forth by the police and adopted by the members have unified the activities of Chicago's Citizen Radio Patrols. The police in their wisdom, however, have left each patrol the flexibility to organize and function in its own way, based on individual personalities and the differing needs of local communities.

**Assessment of Lakeview Radio Patrol.** The Lakeview Radio Patrol and the Chatham Park Manor Patrol were singled out for review here, not because one group is white operating in a primarily white community and the other is black operating in a black community, but because of differences in reasons for beginning and approaches to the solution of similar problems. Crime in both areas reached a level highly objectionable to residents. The degree of citizen concern has always been about equal.

*Organizational Viability.* Let us briefly summarize the viability and relationships of one of the patrols. Of the two groups, the Lakeview Radio Patrol seems more "professional," according to police, and probably more effective. An officer of the Business and Youth Crime Prevention Section said, "If you want to look at the best one, look at Lakeview." Perhaps the fact that this group was formed out of mutual concern for citizen band radios accounts for their success and membership interest.

Personalities play little role in the functioning of this group. In fact, no one at police headquarters seems certain which member is president. All members seemed to have assumed equal responsibility for and interest in keeping the operation going efficiently.

There is virtually no turnover in membership, and they make no effort to restrict members to local residents. Anyone who meets their criteria can volunteer. "CB'ers" from as far away as Skokie, a northern suburb, have volunteered and gone out on patrol. Recruitment is usually done on the basis of knowledge in the use of radios and interest in this specialized activity. So far only two or three of the younger members have lost interest and dropped out.

*Police Relationships.* Because of their professionalism and interest in crime detection and prevention, the patrol's relations with the district police have been outstanding. Officer Richard Spiegel has shown his enthusiasm for their activities by working with them on his own time. The patrol displays great sensitivity in maintaining rapport with the police as indicated by the care shown in relaying information. "We are careful of what we relay so the beat officer does not have to come and make out a report for nothing," says one of the members. However, there are still individual street officers who seem to resent the patrol's activities and involvement in police work. In certain cases members are harassed, and their police identification cards are virtually useless with some officers. Yet, on the whole relations are good. The Lakeview Radio Patrol is not in the business of community organizing, nor does it seek support or recruit members from any of the existing community organizations in the area. By remaining somewhat isolated, the patrol has managed to achieve its goals free of any political interference.

There have been attempts by local politicians and world-be politicians to use the Citizen Radio Patrols and certain other groups to illustrate support for law and order. Lakeview, among others, has been approached for these purposes but has managed to avoid exploitation.

*Crime Reduction.* It is difficult to determine whether the patrol has been instrumental in reducing crime. Members cite specific instances where they were responsible for the apprehension of criminals and can verify their claims with newspaper clippings. Cases vary widely. For example, they have been instrumental in such things as the arrest of a man impersonating a police officer, finding a lost child, isolating a wild dog, locating stolen cars, and reporting a variety of crimes; they are especially proud of their successes in spotting and breaking up neighborhood gang activities.

The nature of the police crime reporting system and the fact that the patrol sees to it that crimes *are* reported, make assessment of the total picture difficult. Nonetheless, the fact that the former district commander utilized the patrol to cover sensitive, high-crime areas when cars were down and regular police workforce was inadequate verifies the value of their activities. There is now a new commander in the 19th district, and it is too early to evaluate current relationships.

## Mobile Patrol: Compton, California

Compton's experience offers a number of valuable lessons in leadership, aggressiveness, and police relationships. This kind of leadership, although dynamic, made police officials apprehensive because it led the volunteers to assume some official police duties and bypass sworn officers in certain arrests. This has hurt relationships with the police department. On the other hand, aggressiveness had led to unusual arrests and program effectiveness.

**Organization.** California Community Alert Patrol (CCAP), founded in 1965, is an organization of roughly 200 active volunteers, centered around the use of mobile patrols and citizen band radios. Each volunteer buys his/her own CCAP jacket and uses his/her own car and gas. Most donate a couple hours of time per month, while some patrol every day. Some foot patrolling is done around schools. A ground-floor apartment adjacent to police headquarters serves as the CCAP office and club house.

CCAP states that there are over 5,000 persons in the Compton area with FCC licenses, many of whom hold membership in Community Alert. Since CCAP is a community service group, members are eligible for a tax write-off on equipment, and they also get a chance to use their gear officially since ideal "chit-chat" is not allowed on the citizen band. These incentives tend to attract members to the organization.

The male-female ratio of adult volunteers is about 50:50. Ages are mostly 35 to 50 years and older, and women serve in the patrols too. On paper there is a board of directors, but no one can seem to recall a meeting. In actuality, Ganzia Washington, CCAP's former "commander in chief" (military titles are used by the organization) who has since left town, had a free hand when he led the group. "He did not answer to anyone and was not elected to this position," say some former top-level participants who dropped out because of disagreements over leadership. "No meetings are ever called to lay out plans in his group – he was the show."

**Purpose and Activities.** The official purpose stated in the by-laws is fourfold: (1) Search and rescue (to seek and find lost or kidnapped children), (2) emergency radio service for public safety in the event of an "act of God or civil disaster," (3) police-community relations, and (4) service to young adults (mainly in the area of juvenile delinquency).

Although it performs these functions, its major emphasis is on mobile patrolling. Vehicles are clearly marked with CCAP's insignia. Chief Thomas Cochee concluded that the association's "primary objective is to act as a citizen surveillance patrol and to alert the police department on in-progress criminal activities." CCAP members call in suspicious activities to their own base on two-way radios, and the base passes the information to the police department. A 24-hour hotline is available for citizens who wish to remain anonymous; over 20,000 residents have been issued CCAP membership cards and decals with the hotline number.

There have been times when CCAP members waded into the thick of battle between gangs. To some the risk of getting hurt has held a certain pride. They can recall only one serious injury when a member was shot six times in an effort to remove a bomb planted by radicals during a church meeting involving a school crisis. Members claim that no volunteers were lost because of the shooting. As a matter of fact, they say, it strengthened their resolve.

It is against the rules to carry weapons, a problem at the beginning of the program. In no uncertain terms, police made their position clear initially against the use of firearms and largely resolved the problem. But CCAP members, mostly for effect, make it clear to gangs that they do have weapons available. Nevertheless no firearms have actually been used, according to CCAP's leaders.

The police department has cooperated to a reasonable degree. They regularly alert CCAP of homes where people are on vacation or where special area problems exist, such as large numbers of burglaries, gang harassment, graffiti nuisance, etc. Window cards announcing "this property is being protected by CCAP" are also distributed.

Duties vary. If a home is broken into, CCAP will send a volunteer to sit in the house until the owner returns. CCAP has fought off a gang to protect an elderly couple. They patrol shopping center parking lots, and they believe that their mere presence in patrol areas has stopped purse snatching, theft of groceries, muggings, and other incidents. They snap pictures of offenders, relay license numbers, and plot direction of offenders in flight. Internal store security is also one of their roles.

**Junior Patrol.** Interestingly, CCAP has organized a junior-patrol which focuses on school security and petty thefts, beatings, and other incidents involving youth. Young members are also very good at finding lost or run-away children. Decals identify homes where a child may go in case of an emergency.

**Delinquency Prevention.** Philosophically, CCAP sees itself as a major deterrent to juvenile delinquency. Ganzia Washington, CCAP's former "commander in chief," observed: "What we'd like to see — if there's a chance for this boy to change, we'd like to have him paroled out to us, and have us put him in CCAP, or try to find him a job." There is a noticeable thrust to institute goals aimed primarily at the city's male delinquents. There is a "save our male resources" tone, an urge to guide young men into productive life.

**Grantsmanship.** For several years Ganzia Washington and CCAP tried to get some government funding, but without results. Recently some members were funded to work closely with the police department; however, a more comprehensive proposal calling for some $325,000 in personnel and $82,000 in equipment expenditures never materialized. Washington complained about the funding of all types of "useless" studies and projects and no money for a "sincere and direct involvement" project like his own that deals "with real problems."

Although the proposal calls for overly ambitious goals, some residents would like to see CCAP given a chance to prove themselves, and CCAP leaders believe that they can substantially and realistically reduce crime. The stated goals are as follows: (1) reduce home burglary and home defacement; (2) reduce business and shopping thefts; (3) establish two 20-person patrols on staggered 10-hour shifts on the streets most of the time; (4) install two-way radios on all business properties and in senior citizen homes to monitor crimes in progress; (5) promote special porch lights to alert CCAP patrols in case of emergency; (6) secure moving pictures and positive identification of persons defacing property; (7) maintain two junior CCAP offices in vacant houses for members 7 to 12 and 13 to 19 years of age; and (8) patrol around every school.

Law enforcement officials believe that if CCAP could accomplish part of what they say they can, the money would be well spent. But city officials were always worried about Ganzia Washington's credibility and were not sure of his abilities or sincerity. In the face of not getting funded and with all the delays and uncertainties, Washington departed south to another state to take up his crusade. CCAP still functions but in a much lower key than previously.

## Mobile Alabama's Community Watch

Mobile has 260,000 people and is still growing, while many other urban cores are declining in population. Burglary is one of the most serious crimes, encouraged by the easily accessible and insecure old homes. Violent crime is not as serious as in most urban areas, and people walk the streets at all hours, usually without fear, except for particular hubs where drug traffic exists. Mobile's south-westerly location makes it easier for thiefs to fence stolen goods out-of-the-state.

Volunteer crime prevention groups are sponsored and trained through the Police Department's Public Relations Division, supervised by two rabid optimists, Lieutenant Tom Nelson and Officer Alex Zavros, who believe in bringing out the most and best in citizens. After a burglary they say, "lightning hits the citizen," and he or she wants to do something. They help to organize and train interested volunteers.

**Mixed Racially**. The most successful civilian patrol, the 150-member Community Watch, started six years ago. It began as an all-black organization in an area known as "little Hell's Kitchen" and has grown to include all areas of the city with members from widely varied educational and economic backgrounds. The black-white ratio is about 50:50, and cooperation has reached all races and economic groups for the first time — quite notable for a Deep South city. But there is a "home town" attitude here, where inhabitants take intense pride in being local citizens.

A formidable organization, Community Watch has the respect and full cooperation of the entire police department.

**Equipment**. Community Watch is amazingly well equipped for a volunteer group, partially because of the availability of city funds and partially through the Public Relations Division's resourcefulness in acquiring material second-hand from the police. Members wear uniforms similar to sworn police — gray shirt, blue pants, and a bright patch with the same city symbol used on regular uniforms. Cars are owned by the volunteers, who pay for gasoline and upkeep themselves, and vehicles are marked with magnetic signs to make them readily identifiable. Many cars are equipped with large fire extinguishers, tanks of oxygen, gas masks, yellow revolving light, and switch for extra-bright headlights. Sirens are on the forbidden list.

Each is equipped with a citizen band radio, and the Community Watch operates on Channel 14, with Channel 10 as an alternate or "10-32" channel for long-winded conversations. It is interesting to hear this same channel used by truck drivers who transmit such things as, "Whatcha say, got a 16-wheeler eastbound on 1-10, Smokey's got his clock out at Broad Street and he is collecting green stamps, so light on the hammer, boys." Community Watch officers are trained in the same local signals as regular police, including the international or "ten" code used worldwide.

**No Weapons Allowed.** The one forbidden object in the Community Watch is the gun, although some carry "Sheriff," a drugstore deterrent milder than mace. The purpose of the Community Watch is the same as other mobile units and block associations — to be the eyes and ears of the police. Among a small minority, human weakness and the desire for personal protection have caused some Community Watch officers to carry weapons secretly. One incident occurred when two Community Watch officers inadvertently walked in on a robbery in progress at a convenience store. The bandits, thinking they were being confronted by real police, opened fire, and one Community Watch member pulled his gun, wounding both suspects and ultimately causing their arrest. In the course of the exchange, the volunteer was slightly wounded himself from shotgun pellets in the leg. This caused quite a quandary for the police department, which was inclined to praise and reprimand him simultaneously.

**Organization and Training.** The city is divided into eighteen general areas, each with a "base station" usually operated by the wife of a Community Watch officer. All officers operate in their own neighborhoods, although some are given the general "run of town" beat, working in areas where special concentration is needed. A main station is located atop a ten-story building near the center of the city, and Officer Zavros has a station in his Dauphin Street home which monitors all activities.

Obviously, such a program requires careful screening of potential members. Fingerprinting, criminal and traffic records, medical history, possible drug usage, and educational level are some of the more intimate details of a person's life which are investigated. Training, with assistance from the Police Academy, involves several elements: the law and what constitutes crime or a situation worthy of calling the blue-and-white; basic first-aid and emergency care; auto safety and general maintenance; radio language and proper usage; and common-sense street psychology in which regular police are trained. By the time a Community Watch officer finally gets a uniform, the police department expects him to be of proven trust and loyalty. The Community Watch requires such a commitment that few who join ever quit, and most take deep pride in membership.

Rank in the Community Watch follows that of regular police: major, captain, lieutenant, sergeant, and officer. Ranks are designated on uniforms in the same way as on regular police outfits.

Most of the officers are between the ages of 21 and 40 and are male heads of families. Zavros adds this interesting note: "Often we have a man whose wife thinks he's joining just to get out of the house, and in a matter of weeks, she's at his side riding, or operating a base station. We have many excellent husband-wife teams now." The radio will often describe it this way: "Car 132, put me 10-7 [out of service] in about ten. Coming home, honey, I love you" — the kind of transmission one rarely hears on regular police radio and, of course, is not expected to.

**Activities**. Meetings are held in the Police Academy, and they concentrate on what to watch for in particular areas or on special nights. Discipline training is also part of the program. Nominal fines of 25¢ and $1 are handed out for such things as improper use of the radio, going out of beat areas, asking for regular police when unnecessary, and improper uniform. The money is put in a sick/injury kitty.

Patrols vary in the interest generated. Many nights go by without anything happening. "After all, if nothing is going on," said volunteer Mike Hartman, "I feel our presence is already being felt." Other evenings involve incidents of drug pushing, loitering gangs, fires, drunken drivers, speeders, following up on burglar alarms, spotting thiefs on roofs and in back alleys, and a host of illegal activities. Police are summoned in most of these cases. And more volunteer help is needed. The one weakness pointed out by Lieutenant Nelson is that a city of this size needs a volunteer force of close to 300 — or twice the present membership.

Much of the Community Watch's activities center around straight public relations activities. They own a bus which provides tours to citizen groups from within and outside the city. Guides describe the history of Mobile and points of interest and beauty, all subtly interspersed with community relations talk. Most notable of these bus runs are those which service the elderly to group functions, polling places, and other activities. The drivers volunteer their own time as guides and aides.

The Community Watch also helps organize and train sports teams through the Police Athletic League (PAL). Participants in the league are mostly local blacks of all ages, and the main concern is to provide recreational outlets for the young. Nelson describes the sly psychology in using blue-and-white uniforms for all PAL-sponsored teams which participate in city recreation programs: "We try to convince the kids that they can't call us 'pigs,' simply because once they put on our colors, they're the pigs, too. Somehow the association between uniforms and sponsors works well, and we can safely say our programs have kept many a potential troublemaker from ending up on our docket books."

**Other Volunteer Groups**. Other volunteer groups operate in Mobile besides the

Community Watch. Dominant among these are the Police Reserve and the CBs of South Alabama. Both are used primarily during holiday periods, particularly the volatile Mardi Gras celebrations. On these occasions they operate pretty much the way Community Watch does, but do not stop and question people or carry as much equipment. The Police Reserve — many of whom are full-time private security guards — also functions as volunteer security for private affairs and traffic handling at concerts and football games. The Sheriff's Flotilla, a 70-member volunteer search and rescue group, assists in boating and swimming accidents, which outnumber homicide deaths in summertime 2 to 1 because of the many miles of waterway.

*New York City*

We have already discussed New York City's matching fund program. Much of it is used to support mobile patrols too. The police department reports that over 100 civilian groups patrol the neighborhoods and are composed of 11,000 volunteers engaged in foot patrols and 1,800 in mobile patrols. The mobile activity takes place in 23 different precincts, primarily in the outlying areas of the city, which are comprised of one- and two-family homes and some apartments. In the older inner city and more densely populated sections, tenant foot patrols predominate because more crimes take place inside buildings than on the streets. Since motorized units cover a great deal more ground, they are more valuable in areas less dense and with scattered housing.

Patrol requirements are strict. No weapons are permitted. No red or blue lights, sirens, or unusual horns may be used, and all traffic regulations must be obeyed. Logs of calls are kept. Importantly, patrols must be conducted with a minimum of two persons.

Methods are similar to patrols in other cities, and effectiveness varies from one area to the other, depending primarily on the ability of organizations to recruit members and hold their interest.

In Jamaica (Queens), interest in patrolling varies a great deal. Most of the time it is difficult to round up volunteers; thus the burden usually falls on six to ten regulars. But at other times as many as nine patrols operate (each covering about five square blocks), as interest increases or because of an encouraging contact from the area leader.

The Crime Prevention Unit in Jamaica reports that the program is "very good," but they would like to see it expanded and better organized. Even when operating one day a week during the high-crime periods, police say the patrols are very beneficial.

Another unit in Queens, Laurelton Safety Patrol, began in 1969 because citizens got tired of vandalism and purse snatchings. It fields as many as 14 autos per night with radios and is composed of 70 members. Results were astonishing during this period, according to patrol leaders. Reported crime decreased 30 percent, said Douglas Cole, who heads the patrol. On the other hand, as crime went down, so did interest; now the patrol only has about 40 members, of whom just 10 are considered active.

Most of the city's civilian patrols do remain active. As long as crime persists at a high level, volunteers will be needed and their interest will remain. Encouragingly, both police and residents report a drop in crime in the areas where citizens are active and where patrols operate.

## Knoxville, Tennessee

It is only in recent years that Knoxvillians became aware of the need to assist police actively in crime prevention. Traditionally local residents have remained independent of any type of involvement on a community basis and have generally treated another person's crime problem as his or her own. Things have changed, and Knoxville has one of the most effective mobile patrols in the country.

About 177,000 people reside in this city of 77 square miles. The 300-person police department is assisted by the University of Tennessee Safety and Security Service in the university area. A number of community crime prevention programs started operations in the past few years, but only one remains – the Christenberry Heights Community Volunteer Patrol Squad.

**Christenberry Heights.** Christenberry Heights is a low-income government housing development of 1,500 inhabitants established in the late 1960s. William Powell, director of the human resources branch of the administrative agency for governmental housing – Knoxville's Community Development Corporation – has been a leader in helping to establish crime prevention programs. He points out that each community has different crime prevention needs because of diversified environmental conditions and feelings about the neighborhood. Socially, educationally, and economically, persons in the subsidized housing projects are about the same, but housing conditions make a difference. Christenberry Heights, for example, is a contemporary and uncluttered housing design with more space for recreation and other facilities than Austin Homes (another government housing project where Powell tried to set up a program), which is an older, more dense environment without open space or sufficient social service facilities.

**Austin Homes.** The Austin Homes, which was built in the 1940s, is extremely congested, a drab environment which residents are not particularly proud of. "For a successful program," Powell says, "you need to have community pride – someone who'll say this is a good place to live and I'm going to keep it this way." Community leaders feel the main reason for failure in Austin Homes was lack of community pride while the reason for success in Christenberry Heights is care and respect for the neighborhood.

**Montgomery Village.** Program failure occurred in a third government housing area, Montgomery Village. Ineffectiveness was primarily due to lack of community interest and leadership, according to Powell. "We had a potentially explosive situation out there, and we still do. But we just couldn't get the people involved. We had no real leadership," he says. Second, some men wanted to carry arms. "A program like this needs to support the police department, not to take the place of the police. We just need one police chief and one good, sophisticated law enforcement agency," Power emphasizes.

Those interested in Montgomery Village were the wrong types. "After runnings a records check . . . . I think it was something like 19 out of 23 had arrest records, and some of them were convicted felons," said Chuck Storey, Knoxville Police Department Information Officer. Another problem, he says, was that some thought patrol would be like television's "Adam-12." Moreover, residents seemed to resent police presence here.

The Chief of the Knoxville Police Department, Joseph Fowler, fully supports community programs but adds this warning for those starting programs anywhere in the city: "I feel these programs provide a definite service to Knoxville, and we will do everything within our power to keep these organizations. I do believe, however, that when these programs are organized, careful consideration should be given to those persons selected to participate. They should act only as the eyes and ears of the police department. And it should be understood that they have no police power whatsoever."

### Methodology in Christenberry Heights

*Leadership and Pride.* Success in Christenberry Heights came about for several good reasons — interest, leadership, and community pride. As a newer community, Christenberry's environment is more pleasing, a factor in community pride; on the other hand, Montgomery Village is a new government development in the same area, and its crime prevention program failed. More than new homes, leadership is a principal factor for success.

"The only thing I can say is that if people in other projects were as serious as those in Christenberry Heights, then their programs would also be successful," Lieutenant Edward Cummings says.

Considerable organizational leadership for this community was provided by Teresa Suman, a social worker with the Community Development Corporation. "What makes a program successful is how much you're willing to give in the preparation," she says. In the beginning, goals were established for a better community and then continually reinforced. The crime prevention proposal was "short and sweet": two men out each night with armbands, flashlights, and note-pads. No weapons except mace. Weekday hours from 8 to 12 P.M. and weekends 8 P.M. to 2 A.M. A 10 P.M. curfew for those 12 years of age and below and 11 P.M. for older youth. The community then voted on it and gave their approval.

Patrols use a van truck and two walkie-talkies purchased from the community's nonprofit store. A base station is located in the community's headquarters that relays emergencies directly to the police. Residents are asked not to call police unless they are really needed. "In many cases, like a child throwing a rock, we don't need to tie up the police," said Suman. "It's a community problem, not a police problem, and the community should try to solve it. "We've actually asked the police not to come in here. But if we do call them, we mean business."

*Grievance Committee.* Another important aspect of the program is a civilian grievance committee which gives back-up support to the patrol but also deals with complaints against the police department and police complaints against residents. Committee appointments are made as follows: two residents are appointed by the community's task force, one is appointed by the police department, one is chosen from outside the community, and one is nominated by the Welfare Department or Social Service Agency.

Complaints signed against youths by the patrol come before the board, and parents are brought in to help determine how to prevent future occurrences. As parents realize the program's benefits to the community from the local publicity generated by it, they are more willing to cooperate. The board can recommend that a family be evicted for good reason, and the housing authority seriously considers the board's actions. This attention given to the board makes it more powerful in the eyes of the residents, resulting in greater cooperation. For those parents who do not cooperate, the next step is referral to a police juvenile officer, which parents like to avoid.

**Maintaining Volunteer Effectiveness.** Motivating patrol members in Knoxville is apparently not a big problem. "I think you would find this problem more predominant in the upper classes," speculates Teresa Susman. "They probably feel that [patrolling] is something that might be a little bit beneath their dignity. Our people have never really accepted responsibility in their lives. Perhaps it's because of their limited awareness process. But now our program seems to have awakened them to responsibility, and they like it. Their kids respect them because they know that their parents are out there trying to help them have a better life. . . . It's our goal to have our kids become good, contributing citizens."

# 4

## Effect of Block Clubs and Mobile Patrols on Crime and Police

### Effect on Crime

Evidence exists that block associations have had a positive effect on reducing crime. In some neighborhoods where crime declined, the only recognizable change was the formation of block clubs, while police workforce, deployment of forces, technical innovations, and other factors remained relatively constant. This occurred while crime rates were rising in these cities as a whole.

The methodology used to determine the effect of community organization on crime included three elements: (1) statements from both community leaders and police officials, (2) review of local evaluation reports and comparison of crime rate statistics before and after block organizations were created, and (3) survey sampling of block club leaders.

Community leaders and police officials have been fairly uniform in their belief that both crime and fear have been reduced because of block club organization and more active involvement of citizens in police activities. Experiences from individuals as well as from groups in block club meetings support these claims. Interviews of ex-offenders by staff from the Block Association of West Philadelphia, for example, show that block club activity "definitely frightens off professional criminals." On the other hand, the amateur offender is less likely to know or to make the effort to learn about organized citizen activity.

Some of the reasons for reduction in crime are attributed to increased citizen alertness and reporting of crimes, more responsive police in areas where block clubs function, better home and property security, and the presence of community activities — such as neighborhood walks and patrols, meetings and workshops, use of warning devices, and other techniques — which tend to discourage the criminal element or cause them to operate elsewhere. Block captains say the word gets out that a particular area is not a "cool place" to commit crime; as a result, crime may shift to other areas. Some police officials believe that this is all the more reason for citizens to form block clubs in every section of the city.

In West Philadelphia, crime reduction has had much to do with an increase in property values and the desire of people to live in the area.[a] In this regard, *Realty Roundup* reported that "Much of the credit can go to . . . the Block

---

[a]Jack Smyth, "Neighbors Urged to Unite in Battling Crime," *Philadelphia Evening Bulletin,* March 4, 1973.

Association of West Philadelphia." During BAWP's first year, property values jumped 51.3 percent compared to 12 percent for the rest of the city. This is all the more impressive, says Oscar Teller, when one realizes that West Philadelphia was "ready to give up the ghost."[b]

## Examples of Local Experience

Reviews of several cities show reductions in crime as a result of citizen involvement.

**Oakland: Criminal Justice Evaluation of Community Project.** Oakland attributes significant reduction in crime to its Police-Community Cooperation Project. Crime increased steadily throughout the 1960s; finally in 1970 the upward spiral of serious offenses was broken. That year eneded with 7.4 percent fewer FBI Crime Index offenses than had been reported in 1969. Particularly gratifying, auto theft dropped 19 percent; robbery, 3 percent; and burglary, nearly 3 percent. Of great significance, residential burglary — the prime target of Home Alert (association of block clubs) — decreased nearly 2 percent, the first reduction in that offense which had been recorded in more than a decade.[c]

Funding for the Police-Community Cooperation Project terminated in March 1971. That same year burglary rose by 2.7 percent, robbery by 7.1 percent and auto theft by 15 percent. Oakland's evaluation report stated:

As distressing as the early 1971 serious crime increases were, it would be invalid to conclude that the Police-Community Cooperation Project had been a failure. It is impossible to estimate what the crime rate in Oakland would have been had it not been for the project and the efforts of thousands of citizens who, for the first time, came forward to voice their concern for crime and their willingness to do what they could to protect themselves and their neighbors. Certainly, their efforts were a primary force in the deceleration of the spiraling crime rate which Oakland has suffered for years.[d]

Although crime in Oakland rose in 1971, many of the Home Alert areas experienced declines in burglaries. The project "was an unquestioned success" in informing citizens of their responsibilities and encouraging them to take steps to protect themselves and their property, according to the report. It concludes:

---

[b]Oscar Teller, "University City Today, Real Estate Roundup," *The Philadelphia Inquirer,* March 10, 1973.

[c]*The Oakland Police-Community Cooperation Project,* California Council of Criminal Justice, Grant No. 70-DF 115, C. R. Gain, Chief of Police, Oakland Police Department, July 1, 1971. Section 4-1.

[d]Ibid., Section 4-2.

The significance of making so many persons aware of crime conditions and crime prevention methods is at least three-fold: First, for thousands of Oakland residents crime is no longer a nebulous, ill-defined threat; it has been brought into a proper perspective and identified as a problem with which the police and citizens, working together, can cope. Second, the programs have brought the police and thousands of persons into contact in an atmosphere of mutual assistance and congeniality and, for many persons, the police are no longer anonymous faces in an occupying force. Citizens have learned to work together to protect each other and the spirit of participation and self-help has carried over to make community living a more pleasant experience. Home Alert members have become acquainted with their neighbors, many for the first time, and they have engaged in such community activities as clean-up campaigns, neighborhood dances and other social events. Finally, the programs have served to harden many criminal targets. A random sample disclosed that 67 percent of the persons who became involved in Home Alert have taken steps to better secure their property but it will never be known how many persons have effected the simple crime prevention measures set forth in the newsletters and in the various crime prevention brochures which were distributed widely throughout the community.[e]

**Recent Results with Home Alert.** Because of the success of police-community cooperation efforts, Oakland continued to promote Home Alert with its own resources even after federal funds were exhausted. A nine-person security unit still promotes and maintains Home Alert, and they are enthusiastic about the success of community organization. The unit cites 1974 major crime statistics that show reductions of as much as 50 percent in areas where citizens have been intensely organized and joined in cooperating with the police. In the 29th police district, for example, the security unit states that, under the leadership of Mrs. Gus Blakely, the district experienced a complete reversal in its crime figures from the third highest of twenty-nine beats in major crimes to twenty-fourth. Residents agree. They say there was a 90 percent chance of "getting ripped off here; now it has reversed." Other areas, too, report remarkable improvements.

*Robbery and Citizen Assistance.* Officers not intimately associated with community prevention efforts are prone to credit crime reduction to almost anything other than citizen involvement. Yet street officers who work with citizen groups on the "front line" and recognize the times witnesses have identified offenders and have served as eyes and ears for police are willing to credit citizens for their effectiveness.

Recent, interesting findings demonstrating the need for citizen assistance in robbery prevention have come out of a three-year study completed for Oakland, entitled *The Prevention and Control of Robbery*. Immediate assistance from citizens and citizen identification were considered highly important ingredients — more so than confessions, physical evidence, and certain other factors:

---

[e]Ibid., Section 4-3.

1. Most robbery apprehensions are made as the result of immediate action by citizens and the police; between 60 and 90 percent in most cities. Detectives and follow-up investigations are rarely as central to the apprehension process as is commonly thought.
2. Half of all robbery suspects caught in Oakland are arrested either at the scene of the crime or in the immediate vicinity. Two-thirds are arrested at the scene, in the immediate vicinity or are known to the victim.
3. Identification evidence is by far the most important kind of evidence for charging robbery suspects.
4. Confessions are relatively unimportant, being judged as essential for only 5 to 10 percent of the charged suspects.
5. Physical evidence is rarely important in robbery cases.[f]

The study also found that most robberies occur in rather limited geographic areas and to older persons. The two most intense areas of robbery were skid row, late-hour bars, and prostitution districts. In the city as a whole, two-thirds of the half-block-size areas had no robberies or purse snatching at all. On the other hand, 25 percent occurred in 4 percent of the half-block-size areas and over 50 percent along 36 major streets; almost three-fourths of the robbers committed the offenses in their own towns and 42 percent of the individual robbers in their own neighborhood. Moreover, it was found that robbers prey heavily on the old and helpless; over half of the victims were over 65 years of age. For all ages, physical resistance generally led to injury while screaming brought no adverse reaction and occasionally helped.[g]

An analysis of these findings indicates that for some areas block organization for crime prevention purposes would be useful and particularly beneficial for the aged. Whistles or freon horns would probably help also. In any case, citizen cooperation for identification of offenders is an important and invaluable resource. The usefulness of these additional eyes and ears for watching homes and preventing burglaries is certainly as significant and even more so in areas where burglary is the most frequent crime.

**Los Angeles.** Los Angeles provides another excellent experience for both crime and fear reduction as the result of citizen involvement. The city reported that the crime rate from 1964 through 1971 was a steady, annual increase: 1965, 11 percent; 1966, 6.5 percent; 1967, 8.1 percent; 1968, 11 percent; 1969, 3.5 percent; 1970, 4.5 percent; and 1971, 4.8 percent. In 1972 and 1973, when community involvement was swinging into high gear, the rates dropped 3.9 percent and 6.6 percent, respectively. For the first half of 1974, Los Angeles had a 2.6 percent crime increase while the nation was experiencing a 15 percent increase.

And in regard to at least one spectacular result, the tip from a citizen led to

---

[f]Floyd Feeney and Adrianne Weir, *The Prevention and Control of Robbery,* The Center on Administration of Criminal Justice, University of California, Davis, February 1974, pp. 5–8.

[g]Ibid.

the discovery of the Symbionese Liberation Army hideout and subsequent shootout. If there had not been a community involvement program in that area, believes Lieutenant Frank Isbell, there would have been no tip.

In 1974, attendance at various types of community participation meetings totaled 346,789. According to Chief Edward Davis, the department hopes to have its Neighborhood Watch program citywide during 1975. Through the analysis of local crime statistics and the reaction of police officers, Chief Davis credits community involvement with at least half the decline in the city's crime rate. One of his police detectives who had been on the force for ten years said, "Community involvement could virtually wipe out burglaries, but not everybody's involved." Chief Davis is trying to get everybody involved.

*The Venice Experience.* The Venice area is representative of Los Angeles as a whole: 85 percent Caucasian, middle to low income, and a mixture of industrial and residential areas. It covers 3 square miles and has a population of 36,000.

It has several distinct communities: Westchester, upper-middle and middle class; Palms-Mar Vista, middle and lower-middle class; Oakwood, black ghetto and Mexican-American barrio; and the beach area, Bohemian, free-swinging, hippie, politically radical, homosexual, and drug-oriented cultures.[h]

At the end of a 15-month police experiment, statistics showed the following crime reductions: 32 percent in burglaries, 14 percent in robberies, 12 percent in auto thefts, and 21 percent in burglary/theft from vehicles.[i]

Police say community involvement played a major role. In the Team 28 area 50 out of 1,000 crimes were cleared by citizen assistance. The statewide average is 7 in 1,000.[j]

*The Hollywood Experience.* The Hollywood area also contains a cross section of Los Angeles economic and social strata. It has sizable residential areas above and below fabled Hollywood Boulevard. In the hills above it are many expensive homes. Below is an increasing lower-income population.

In the decade preceding 1973, Hollywood experienced an unbroken trend of annual increases in the four most repressible crimes. In 1963, the per capita crime rate in Hollywood was 61 per 1,000 population, compared to 51 per 1,000 for the entire city.

By 1972, both the citywide and Hollywood crime rates had increased, but the gap had almost tripled with 28 more crimes per 1,000 in Hollywood than in the rest of the city. Declining socioeconomic conditions were blamed.

In 1973, crime decreased 11 percent in Hollywood, the first drop in 10

---

[h]*Final Evaluation of Team 28,* Los Angeles Police Department, April 1974.

[i]Ibid.

[j]*Neighborhood Action Team Policing,* Los Angeles Police Department, May 1974.

years, while the city as a whole was experiencing a 7.5 percent drop. Another significant figure during the same year was that attendance at neighborhood crime-suppression meetings increased 225 percent in Hollywood.

Concerning the reversal of the Hollywood crime trend, the police department notes: "The only significant change in police operations was the implementation of a neighborhood-action type of community involvement program."[k]

*The 77th Street Experience.* The 77th Street area, a high-crime neighborhood scene of the Watts riots in 1965, has a predominately black, low- to middle-income population. Neighborhood Watch was formed in 1974, with block captains appointed for most blocks. Decals are used in windows reading "Neighborhood Watch prevents Burglaries."

Estelle Van Meter, a program coordinator, as well as other club members, has noticed a lower crime rate as a result. Block captain Viola Collins said that there have been no burglaries at all on the block in the first 6 months the club was formed. Police statistics verify a decline in crime in the area.

**Knoxville, Tennessee.** The Knoxville experience is limited to one area where citizens are actively involved, and results have been positive. Although crime data are gathered on a citywide basis, the police department has been able to pull out some information manually and make comparisons.

"I think the program has definitely reduced crime in that area [Christenberry Heights]," says Lieutenant Edward Cummings. "I know we're not having the burglaries out there like we used to. In the past, we would get 20 to 30 calls to Christenberry per week. But now, we're only receiving on an average about five calls. And . . . most of the calls received now usually are not serious calls. A lot of them are mental or domestic-related complaints. If you compare Christenberry Heights with other government projects, Christenberry is without doubt the least violent."

Success — expressed by both police and residents working and living in the neighborhood — comes in many ways. A typical explanation is made by Teresa Susman, a community leader:

Take our children [Christenberry Heights] for example. We haven't had an active case in Juvenile Court in nine months. At Gresham Junior High, the principal says our children have the highest attendance as compared with other communities. Vandalism in Christenberry has been way down. In the first nine months of the patrol's operation, vandalism was about $400, as compared to approximately $4,000 in damages in other developments. In the recent garbage strike, people set fires to dumpsters throughout the city, but in Christenberry Heights not one dumpster had to be replaced.

---

[k]Ibid.

**Block Leader Surveys.** A 1974 Center for Governmental Studies survey of 38 block leaders in the West Philadelphia Block Association revealed that almost all felt that both crime and fear had been reduced on their blocks. The sampling of 232 leaders from 900 block clubs in Oakland revealed about the same results.

In Compton, a city of 80,000 persons of whom 98 percent belonged to minority groups, a survey of 44 block club leaders showed that the majority felt crime had been reduced. The surveys drew an average 60 percent response. The results for the three cities are shown in Table 4-1.

**Table 4-1**
**Block Leader Crime Survey of Three Cities**

|  | *Yes* | *No* | *Could not tell* |
|---|---|---|---|
| | *Has it reduced crime?* | | |
| West Philadelphia | 18 | 3 | 5 |
| Oakland | 62 | 24 | 12 |
| Compton | 24 | 1 | 1 |
| | *Has it reduced fear?* | | |
| West Philadelphia | 16 | 6 | 3 |
| Oakland | 32 | 51 | 10 |
| Compton | 15 | 8 | 2 |
| | *Has it been effective?* | | |
| West Philadelphia | 19 | 4 | 1 |
| Oakland | not compiled | | |
| Compton | 22 | 1 | 3 |

Source: Center for Governmental Studies, completed November 1974.

**Effect on Police**

*Negative Reactions*

Police officials started out with skeptical views about block clubs in a number of cities. This has largely changed. Some conceptualized block associations as starting up and phasing out too frequently, with a great deal of effort required for their maintenance. Some clubs caused disfavor because they tried to supplant police authority in a few instances. At least one group started out primarily to investigate police and catch them in actions which could be used against the police department. The backlash from this brought negative reaction from surrounding police departments, and it took considerable persuasion from new block club leaders to convince officials that their purposes were different.

In one case, a patrol group took the law into its own hands. They apprehended offenders and illegally used red flashing patrol lights, and a few carried guns. The atmosphere was certainly vigilante, and police could not trust them until the club leadership and style of operation changed. The police department established strict rules and enforcement procedures in order to prevent abuses. The old civilian leadership was phased out, and new trusted leaders were groomed by the community. Now the association is accepted, although police are still cautious and watchful that it does not revert to its old ways.

Another reason for negative reaction is the fear for loss of jobs; some officers are afraid volunteers might hold down the need for police workforce. But with significant shortages of sworn officers, this fear has proved unfounded. Volunteers' main activities have been to help police reduce crime and demonstrate community concern for crime prevention, so very much lacking in most cities and counties. The need for more police help has never been questioned. Rather than numbers, the main concern now seems to center around police department training and community involvement.

**Positive Reactions.** On the positive side, police have recognized great value in block clubs. In many cases neighborhood groups have been able to reach people alienated by police, get them interested in crime prevention, and rebuild citizen trust in and respect for law enforcement, something which is usually difficult for police to do alone.

In regard to developing better relations with police, block clubs generally have been able to build trust with police by inviting them to club meetings and openly demonstrating their purpose and genuineness in bettering police-community relations. To a large extent, block association meetings and police-citizen interchanges have had greater effect on police image than standard police public relations programs. Many police departments have recognized this value and have promoted the idea of patrol and other police officers meeting and interchanging information directly with resident groups and block club leaders.

Clubs also provide a buffer for police and absorb some of their workload by dealing directly with community law enforcement problems. Associations meet to resolve community crime problems and guide police on neighborhood feelings. They discuss family and general neighborhood disputes, agree on curfew rules, and assist by talking to and providing activities for delinquent youths. Police feel more comfortable in this atmosphere of cooperation, enjoy their work more, and feel safer knowing residents will hold down hostility and assist officers in a "tight spot."

In the development of block associations, police would rather see well-organized, constructive citizen groups created than vigilante types. To ensure that this happens, the police should set aside some of its own resources in workforce and money to assist in the development of legitimate block clubs. If established early enough, legitimate groups can pre-empt vigilante bodies and are certainly more desirable.

As officers have gotten to know residents more intimately, police attitudes and response time have improved. Some clubs keep accurate records of events and log books of police response time. Although unusual police delays are reported to the district captain, relations with the police have actually improved because police efficiency and effectiveness have increased, and both city and police officials have appreciated this benefit. Usually two factors — cooperation and community surveillance — are the reasons for improved police service to the neighborhood.

The attitude of police leaders is important as to how other officers conceive citizen participation. Negative attitudes poison thinking. Officers need to be well versed on the purpose of block clubs, and they should be trained in how to work with citizen groups. Those who are instructed to attend community meetings should be the same officers who patrol the area. They should be briefed on the backgrounds of various organizations, the individuals involved, how to respond to citizen requests, and what to do when hearing a whistle or freon horn. Officers should distribute relevant neighborhood crime information — preferably on a block-by-block basis — and help to interpret its meaning and join in community crime prevention planning. They should also be taught how to assist crime victims and elicit their support in future neighborhood activities.

It is this close contact, candor, and full communication that has improved the public's attitude toward police. And it is the hardwork and sincerity of block groups and their desire to assist law enforcement agencies that have caused police to praise club members and feel more comfortable about their own jobs too. If there were no other reasons, these new cooperative relationships between citizens and police are sufficient justification for continued community organization. The building of a sense of community, reduction in crime and fear, a buffer between police and neighborhood problems, a climate for an improved image of law enforcement, and the means for police to be able to reach many more residents than before are all good reasons for community development.

**Steps for Better Police-Community Relations.** Some very basic steps are suggested for police departments to use in developing proper police-community relations through the block association concept:

1. Recognize the existence of community groups and block associations. Keep a record of their purposes, membership, and other information which will help in instructing police officers as to the nature of these bodies.
2. Request meetings with these groups and provide lectures on a regular basis to inform citizens of current police statistics, procedures, and

solutions. This can be done through the police community relations section or a special police unit established for this purpose.

3. Assign responsibility to beat patrol officers and other neighborhood officers to meet with residents daily and with each crime prevention group at their regular meetings. Officers should try to get to know the names of every family on their beat, recognize problem families and delinquent youths, and call families together in smaller meetings periodically. At these small meetings or "coffee klatches," the beat patrol officer gets to know individual family members better and is able to recognize future block club leaders as well. Block problems are discussed, such as block crime rates, recent crime events, recreation facilities, neighborhood half-way house, vacant housing problems, drug traffic, families planning to go on vacation, method of property security, street lighting, noise problems, traffic congestion, and any neighborhood problem of interest. Together police and residents plan and attempt to arrive at solutions.

4. Create a special unit to coordinate and develop block clubs. Crime prevention pamphlets, monthly newsletters, radio and television and newspapers, and personal visitation should be used to promote community involvement. Regardless of which police department division is assigned the responsibility for block club development and maintenance, the specially oriented unit described above should function within the structure.

5. Determine who the natural community and block leaders are and develop their expertise and interest. Special training seminars, workshops, role playing, community college courses, and other means should be used to improve resident leadership and effectiveness. In some cases, police and residents should train and learn together. One city's training objectives are as follows:

   a. To develop neighborhood leadership in the techniques and rationale of block safety and community crime prevention

   b. To establish adequate program administration and central coordination of neighborhood groups

   c. To assist organized blocks in developing positive community programs: (1) counseling and personal assistance for crime victims, and (2) job training, housing counseling, and community support during reentry of released offenders into their own communities

   d. To increase knowledge and improve techniques for community walks and patrols, block club organization and maintenance, street safety, home security, and other crime prevention methods

6. The chief of police should issue guidelines, regulations, and memoranda to all police officers on how to deal with community groups, the operation and importance of block clubs, the effect of resident involvement on crime reduction, and the value of community programs to the police

officer. The program needs to be endorsed by both police leaders and city officials.
7. Devise a community participation week where city and police officials promote block clubs. An annual dinner program shouuld consist of awards to outstanding police and resident participants.

**Examples of Local Experience.** In Los Angeles, the percentage of police officers who support in-depth community involvement is high because Chief Edward M. Davis has acclaimed his belief in citizen participation and has directed police officers not only to cooperate with and respond quickly to citizen groups but to help organize and maintain block clubs.

Although Oakland has a successful block association program, only a small percentage of officers have had direct contact with block programs, and much of the remaining force does not realize the significance of community involvement. Chief George Hart is changing these attitudes by training and explanatory directives. Two civilian district leaders, Betty Thorsen and June Norman, would like to see even greater police cooperation and expansion of the block club program.

In Philadelphia, police cooperation is high and citizen participation welcome, yet fear exists that a full-scale, citywide program many become unmanageable and difficult to cope with politically. Some police officials believe citizen demands and oversight may go too far. However, there is no attempt to slow down the development of block clubs. The state's Criminal Justice Commission has approved funds and staffing to expand the block association concept statewide. The training center is located in Philadelphia and the two principal civilian trainers, Ross Flanagan and Ellie Wegener of the Block Association of West Philadelphia, believe the program will expand rapidly and be well accepted by police.

Dallas is a case where several citizen beat committees (out of 50) damaged the city's program because they went far beyond the scope of their activities and got too deeply involved in the political process to suit city officials. Even under these difficulties, about one-third of the original groups are functioning largely under their own power and will. The police department has mixed feelings about how far to get involved in community participation. It will take more experience to convince the police department one way or the other. Meanwhile, thousands of block clubs are operating successfully throughout the nation, and valuable experience is building day by day.

# 5 Special Crime Prevention Projects

## Introduction

Crime occurs under many different cricumstances and for many reasons; therefore almost as many solutions are necessary to prevent it. Many of the crime prevention projects which follow could very well be part of a block association's general plan, but usually special-interest groups are more inclined to organize these more unique efforts. Although discussed separately here, these projects should be part of the police department's or community's total crime prevention program.

Although the street-oriented block association and mobile patrol may be excellent ways to prevent crime for many neighborhoods, they are of less value to people living in high-rise buildings where much of the crime occurs indoors. Special methods are needed to protect workers who must travel late at night, alone, and who are unusually vulnerable to the criminal element. Block groups which function during earlier hours are not much help to these residents, usually older, female workers.

Special programs are also necessary to watch over youngsters during school hours — considerably different periods from those during which block groups normally function. Parent leagues are very effective in this role.

At times it takes youths to be able to deal effectively with other youths. Youth patrols, properly supervised and trained, can make a significant contribution to protecting children during their travels to and from school and in motivating older youths in the respect for law. In many cases loiterers and youth gangs can be effectively handled by well-organized, disciplined, and responsible community youth groups.

In addition, it is not only economical but makes good sense to use existing business and government groups for crime prevention purposes, such as taxi associations, radio-equipped trucking and other mobile business units, civilian radio patrols, and numerous public agency vehicles. Taxis, delivery trucks, and government vehicles travel regularly over the city and are good sources to assist the police. Only limited resources are required to get private and public interest groups to assist in the fight against crime. Successful organization usually requires leadership from an interested civilian or government official, some training of participants, and a system for continually motivating and inspiring the membership.

More formal groups of citizens, either paid or unpaid, some uniformed, adequately trained and integrated within the police department or closely supervised by them, should be used in crime prevention work. This may include auxiliary police and paid full- or part-time civilians who are usually assigned less hazardous police functions. Such projects are well suited for filling the gaps of a comprehensive crime prevention system — the missing links between using sworn police officers and informal, neighborhood volunteer groups. These techniques are also excellent for increasing the productivity level and general effectiveness of police departments.

### High-rise Tenant Security

Our first discussion involves high-rise building security, particularly the need to organize residents within buildings, as compared to block associations which concentrate their efforts on the horizontal plane of the street. Floor captains, newsletters, lectures, hardware security, and many other familiar techniques are used here too. Again, the key to success is motivating and maintaining the interest of participants.

### Terrace Gardens in New York City

In a community in Brooklyn which is 90 percent Jewish, tenants from three apartment buildings (totaling 382 units) have joined protectively together in the Terrace Gardens Block Association. Violent crime here is minimal, but burglaries are among the highest in the city and the offenders are primarily from outside the neighborhood. As usual the older people (in this case 50 years of age and up) are the most active in the organization. Most of them must participate by circumstances, for economically they have little choice of where they can live.

**Budget.** The association makes good use of New York City's matching fund program. In 1974 it collected $3,337 to match with city funds and received $9,024 from the grant program. Almost 100 percent of the families contributed $5 each. The rest of the amount was raised through block parties, raffles, white elephant sales, and other events. In addition, each family is assessed $2 annual membership dues. Some members contribute supplies or are allowed to use the facilities of their employers for printing and duplicating and other services.

**Operation.** Each floor elects a floor captain — 36 in all — whose duties are to motivate and lead and personally ring every doorbell to inform tenants of what is happening. They are the chief contact between tenants and the association's executive board, comprised of five members from each building. There are monthly meetings and a periodic meeting of tenants from all three buildings.

The budget is mainly used for hardware. Members have agreed to place floodlights every 10 feet along the entire street, and the landlord has consented to pay the electric bill. About $6,000 will be used to fence the back of the buildings along the alley and railroad lines — areas of escape for burglars. A mesh lock-gate is planned for the laundry room and barred windows for the ground floor. Double security locks will be used on all apartment doors. Tenants are instructed to watch neighbor's apartments and for strangers in general. No one is supposed to buzz for someone to enter unless that person has been properly identified. Selling items out of apartments is prohibited to discourage strangers, and stickers and notices warn that the buildings are protected.

Safety in the streets is emphasized too. Members make use of warning devices. Because of all this attention police have become especially responsive since they know tenants are organized and well-meaning. In turn, residents praise the improved relations and the devotion of certain crime prevention officers.

### Lincoln Guild Housing Corporation in New York City

The Lincoln Guild project in New York City was spurred on because of the availability of funds from the city's Block Security Program. In this 420-unit building, tenants own their apartments, which cover a full square block in Manhattan's attractive lower 60s. Some $800 in dues brought in $4,200 in city matching funds. And 40 captains (plus their alternates) serve each floor on the 20-story two-section building. The House Council is the block association. It meets monthly and has four cochairpersons (one for each ten floors) to assist the chairperson. About 25 to 35 people attend the average monthly meeting and 50 or more on special occasions. Floor captains make sure that literature is distributed and each tenant contacted whether they attend meetings or not. Tenants feel this is their building, and they show a great deal of pride in it, according to Harriet Marks, president of the guild. Relations with police are excellent and crime minimal here, she reports.

The principal project so far has been the acquisition and installation of an intercom system between each apartment and the front entrance. A wall directory lists apartment call numbers but not their locations, and no one is admitted without identifying himself/herself. The front door is not supposed to be held open for persons wanting to enter behind someone. Each must use his own key, the association says, or "you defeat the whole system." Tradespeople and advertising or political promoters are not permitted access either. Cylinder guards for apartment locks, grates on laundry windows, and lighting for the rear parking area are also part of the program.

These two different but typical high-rise projects demonstrate what is taking place in many parts of New York. Other cities may find the development of similar crime prevention organizations useful too.

**Protecting Employees**

*Maintenance Employees Organize*

Crime is a problem in areas other than residential and for different categories of people. Maintenance Employees Night Protection Alert Corporation (MENPAC) is a variation of the block association designed to protect employees who must travel long distances to their homes in the early morning hours. Its members do not patrol but rather look out for each other and have joined together in a buddy system for protection.

MENPAC is an auxiliary of the Service Employees Union (Local 32J) which represents nearly 15,000 workers (12,000 cleaning women) with their landlords, cleaning firms, and other building owners. Shortly after the white-collar worker goes home in relative safety, cleaning women — mostly elderly — start out to work; they do not leave for home until 11 P.M. or 1 A.M. the next morning, which makes them easy prey for criminals. MENPAC's own research found that almost 500 of their employees were being mugged every year and that the number of unreported cases are even higher. Something had to be done.

Regular police protection was found inadequate in these early morning hours. Moreover, because the percentage of crime is lower during this period, the police department assigns fewer officers — only about 600 for all of New York City, according to MENPAC. And much of their time is spent on service calls, family disputes, fires, tavern brawls, pregnancy and sick calls, and all kinds of radio alerts quite apart from street crime. Furthermore, block association patrols are off the streets during these hours because their focus has always been on the larger number of people arriving home from work much earlier.

**Activities**. The union provides for MENPAC's budget and its staff of one administrator, two field representatives, and two clerks. Literature is mailed to members regularly, and posters are also used to promote the program. Phones are manned until 8 P.M. each night to receive inquiries for assistance or complaint. The staff performs a variety of functions. It helps members who have been victimized to get through the criminal justice system more easily, promotes better-timed surface transportation and improved street and subway conditions, and pursues the elimination of loiterers. They help victims to receive claims from the state's Crime Victims Corporation Board and also from the Workmen's Compensation program. They also give rewards for the apprehension and conviction of anyone who offends a member — $1,000 for most crimes and $5,000 in the case of murder. Records are kept on travel routes, job locations, and places of residence. The record system helps to facilitate a 5-point plan:

1. A buddy system is instituted where each person is assigned someone as a traveling companion and a backup if the first person is absent.

2. Most night workers going home after work arrive in a given area within a span of two hours. Police are alerted to these times and are given the names of the persons who are in travel.
3. Additional surface transportation is provided to cut down walking distance.
4. Night workers are afforded the opportunity to become acquainted with each other. MENPAC research shows that the majority of people polled are in favor of a system of identification of fellow night workers.
5. There is provision for better street lighting and security devices, also better lighting within buildings and in lobbies, hallways, and stairwells.

**Buddy System.** The buddy system promotes the idea of two or more persons meeting and traveling together to and from work. Data show that members traveling together are far less subject to crime. Of those cleaning women who traveled alone, 18 percent were attacked; of those traveling together or who were met or took a cab, only 0.3 percent suffered attacks.[a] By the end of 1974, MENPAC found 51 percent of its members had traveling companions, 9 percent periodic company, and 40 percent traveled alone. The organization is trying to increase companionship. Police are now also regularly alerted when workers travel and when they arrive home.

**Victims.** The elderly are particularly vulnerable to the aftereffects of crime. Many victims experience mental trauma, blood pressure increases, and psychological anxieties. Some women in their seventies work jobs to make ends meet, and they live in an abyss of fear as they step into the same horror every night. Statistics show young offenders as the most violent, for they have maimed and even stomped old people to death. Yet some workers fight back, chase their muggers. A typical example of perseverance is the 70-year-old woman whose hip was broken by a mugger but who went back to work as soon as she could because she did not want to go on charity. Joan Kinnier, a staff supervisor, cites case after case of this sort.

**Results.** Police now support MENPAC, but in the beginning it was different. "When we first started out, we didn't do so well with them [police]," says Albert E. Perry, MENPAC's president. They regarded us as a "fly-by-night" operation which would not last, he says, but our staying power has caused police support to emerge. Relations are good with the police now because MENPAC is cooperative, verifies complaints, and its members appear as willing witnesses.

"Statistically we can't validate our effect," says Joan Kinnier. "We do know our members aren't getting mugged as much . . . and there is less fear."

---

[a]*Maintenance Employees Night Protection Alert Corporation (MENPAC) Booklet,* March 1974.

Members also feel less isolated now, she believes, because they have a place of their own where crime problems can be reported and help provided to them.

## Protecting Children

Protecting children is a facet of crime prevention which elicits many volunteer helpers and much emotion. With proper citizen training and police involvement, these programs can be effective ways for reducing crime and making both parents and children happier and safer in their neighborhoods. Hundreds of parents' safety groups operate throughout the country in both large and small cities. Here we discuss one which has experienced a good deal of success.

### Child Safety Campaign Start-up and Expansion

Sponsored by the Parents League, the Child Safety Campaign began operation in March 1972 in East Harlem (23rd precinct) and expanded to three other precincts (19th, 20th, and 24th) on the east and west sides of Central Park as more resources became available. Although the Parents League is an association of parents who send their children to private schools, the program seeks members from all schools and, of course, watches and benefits all children in the area. It was started because of the intimidation of younger students by older youths and robbery of lunches, money, watches, and other items.

Expansion was made possible through a $40,000 grant from the New York City Criminal Justice Coordinating Council. And now other volunteer groups are being brought into the program. "We have had requests for information from people in other precincts," says executive director Betty Thompson. "Also, we are meeting with the community school boards . . . and others." Surveys to determine interest have been conducted. Counseling is also provided to new groups, and the program now has an office of its own.

The areas served as a mixture of white, black, Asian, and Spanish surnames. Those who patrol range in age from 16 to senior citizens and are divided about evenly between male and female. Mostly men volunteer to patrol in the early morning before they go to work and women in the afternoon. Senior citizens and older high school students fill in the gaps. Each route requires 20 volunteers, in the morning and afternoon 5 days per week for one-hour shifts. At times in the hot summer months and very cold days "when bad guys don't want to get cold," there are no patrols, say the program's leaders.

### Operations

Over 1,000 volunteers have been trained by Officer Joseph Spinella. Furthermore, though some interest has dropped because "not much is happening anymore," most of the groups are sticking with it. Police community service officers have been providing one-hour training sessions on what to watch for and how to report. Vigilante types are rejected, but members are allowed to engage in removing a potential victim from the scene with emphasis on "extracting persons and not apprehending offenders." Each volunteer carries a warning whistle and wears an orange poncho. Monetary contributions were provided by businesses and private individuals. Merchants also participate in the program by watching the streets and allowing the use of their premises for refuge and also daily report filing of incidents, suspicious persons, etc.

Volunteers also report other city needs such as defective traffic lights, vandalized telephones, roving dogs, and other matters. They do not, however, perform as crossing guards.

## Results

Satisfaction with the program is sufficiently high that the Community Affairs Division and civilian directors are promoting it widely; on the other hand, they are having some difficulty holding volunteers because drime in down and "nothing is happening," according to Ellinor Mitchell, former president of the Parents League. Officer Cecil Bryant has told the volunteers, "If you don't see anthing, if nothing happens, you're doing a good job. You have become an effective deterrent." Nevertheless, it is hard to hold volunteers if some activity or interest is not generated.

Top police officials give the program full support. "It wouldn't work if they [officials] weren't behind it," says Bryant. Both police and residents attest to the program's effectiveness; however, few statistics are available to verify the impact on crime. Anyway, "there is a cycle for everything — especially crime," so figures are hard to justify, says Officer Bryant. But he says unequivocally that crimes against children have dropped to nearly zero near the complex where parents are patrolling. Moreover, members have found tht children feel more secure and are better able to resist offenders when they know adults are nearby and ready to help. Because their children are secure, parents are more comfortable too.

## Involvement by Youths

In many cases it takes youths to deal with youths. Working with youth gangs, loiterers, and delinquents may sometimes be best accomplished by engaging some of these same youths or their peers in the understanding of the problem and the desire to improve one's own living environment. Although a variety of youth patrols exist throughout the country, the idea is still unique and requires special adult supervision and concern for long-term success. Where there was money available to operate programs, such as under Model Cities, Summer Youth Employment, Neighborhood Youth Corps, and certain other grants, local officials experimented with programs in many cities. Let us examine one of these groups which proved effective but was later disbanded for other reasons that could have been avoided under proper adult direction.

*Triboro Youth Squad*

One such project used $34,376 of the Turtle Creek Valley Model Cities Program in Triboro, Pennsylvania, to match the $105,168 of LEAA funds from the governor's Justice Commission. It is a valuable lesson in effectiveness, in how former troublemakers and delinquents can successfully operate such a program, and in how the lives of some participants can be changed. Although it is questionable whether the program will be refunded because of the phasing out of Model Cities and a state investigation of irregular use of project funds, local officials believe that the program was effective and that it could have corrected any of its problems.

**Background.** During the summer of 1971, three communities with a combined population of 23,000 in the eastern suburb of Pittsburgh erupted in racial conflict. Blacks and whites fought openly on the main streets of Braddock, North Braddock, and Rankin. Dissension and animosity were brought out mainly because of the Pennsylvania State Board of Education's decision to combine the schools from the three boroughs into one district (the General Braddock School District). Because of the financial depression of the three individual districts, the State Board of Education reasoned that it would alleviaite the conditions if the three were combined, and thus ordered them to merge. This decision precipitated some social disturbances and discontent among citizens of the three neighboring towns, which through the years had been scholastic and athletic rivals.

The first year of the merger (1971) was merely a merger on paper. The three towns retained their separate schools, events, and even had three separate graduations and commencement exercises. This brought on much controversy between the people who were for and those who were against the merger. Those opposed to the merger argued that all three of the school districts were depressed areas and financially insolvent and that the Board of Education had no right to force the three distressed districts to combine. Those in favor argued that although the merger was not to everyone's complete satisfaction, the state ordered it, and since it must be, all academic resources should be distributed equitably throughout the three communities.

In 1972, subsequent to many heated school board and community meetings in which accusations were hurled about mismanaged school funds, the

State Board of Education sent in a "super board" to oversee and guide the twelve members of the local board of the General Braddock schools. Also at about the same time serious damage was done to school property in Braddock and North Braddock from fires in which arson was suspected but never proved.

All the problems were not confined to school property. Merchants in the town reported many cases of theft, and citizens reported incidents of robbery, assault, and mischief by juveniles.

**Organization and Duties.** Shortly thereafter, concerned individuals in the area formulated plans to organize the Triboro Youth Squad. The Youth Squad was conceived by a few people who felt that if the leaders among young people, including former troublemakers in the three communities, would combine into one constructive group, they could relate to all youths of the communities and help law enforcement officials in the three towns suppress the growing problem of juvenile delinquency.

The Triboro Youth Squad began operation on July 10, 1971. Although the Youth Squad was formed around the same time that the General Braddock merger went into effect and many problems occurring in the communities at that time were induced because of the attitudes toward that merger, their function was *not* related only to the school district. In fact, the original squad totaled 45 members (15 from each of the three towns), and most of the members were high school drop-outs and former problem youths in the schools themselves. The 45 young men and women came together to try to put a stop to the senseless vandalism, fighting, and robberies that put a stigma on the communities. When the squad started, there were no funds nor any paid members. Eventually, government funds were made available.

The method of operation is simple. Members patrol on foot or use their own autos. They wear blue jumpsuits and black hats and get paid $2 per hour. The executive director (at $9,000), deputy director (at $8,000) and two associate directors (at $6,500 each) receive higher salaries.

Members perform a variety of duties including serving on panels for drug programs and working with the Rankin and Braddock Volunteer Ambulance Service; some have been quite active with various police and fire companies in the Braddock, North Braddock, and Rankin area. The Youth Squad has been called on to assist in everything from directing traffic during a fire to acting as special police at athletic events and teenage dances.

Some of the Youth Squad members have gone out into better jobs in the field of police work. For instance, George Petrovay, former Youth Squad associate director, is now Chief of Campus Police at Pennsylvania State's McKeesport campus. Charles Wade, who is the present director of the Youth Squad, is also a security officer at Gee Bee's Department store in North Versailles. Bill Boytko, a present officer in the Youth Squad, is also a security guard at a large North Versailles department store, and several members have gotten jobs with Turtle Creek Valley Model Cities.

**Results**. Since its inception and until the summer of 1974, the Youth Squad directly or indirectly assisted in over 2,000 police cases. Police reports indicate juvenile offenses dropped by more than 50 percent during this period. Police Chief John Spisals stated, "I feel the Youth Squad has done a terrific job in helping us with the young people and in many other cases." He admits that with his own force — which has dwindled from 20 to 8 officers — they would be unable to cope with all the juvenile problems. And Ted Wagner, Chief of Police of North Braddock, says, "To me the Youth Squad is tops. I don't believe there is a finer youth group anywhere in the country." Merchants and citizens alike praise it.

On the other side, some school officials have insisted that the Youth Squad work outside school buildings rather than within. And a few people still believe the squad was made up of "mostly hoodlums and troublemakers." But since its inception, negative reaction has fallen off considerably.

On the whole, the program is considered successful, particularly in reducing crime and delinquency problems. Funding and fiscal control matters are other facets which must still be worked out for long-term viability and management success.

## Taxi Patrols

### General

Another type of patrol uses private business and taxi vehicles to report crime to police. Many cities make use of civilian radio patrols in personal autos, and some communities are successfully using radio-equipped government and private trucks and cars to perform as eyes and ears for the police. One of the most unique and successful techniques is the use of taxicabs in the fight against crime. New York's taxi patrol program can serve as a valuable demonstration of this method and the results that could be achieved by almost any community choosing to follow these guidelines.

If city and, particularly, police officials would closely examine this method of volunteer patrol and make the effort to organize, encourage, and sustain its necessary elements, they could very easily double, triple, or multiply in even greater numbers the effective eyes and ears watching the streets. Most cities have too few police vehicles and cannot afford more.

Volunteer patrols can greatly multiply the number of crime prevention vehicles on the road. The tens of thousands of trucks and cabs in New York City, for example, could significantly increase the effectiveness of the police department and its approximately 1,000 police cars which are on the streets at any one time. New York has already made a good start in this direction, and it can be done in any city, of any size. Where police officials fail to respond, fleet owners and volunteer crime prevention groups could very well take the initiative. This is what happened in New York City. Cab owners originated an association, put in their own money, and now sustain the operation. And the New York Police Department has enthusiastically participated in and supported the program.

**Background.** Taxi drivers are in an ideal position to report accidents and crime. "It is because you know the streets of New York so well and are sensitive to their rhythms and danger signals," says Police Commissioner Michael J. Codd, "that you are uniquely able to serve as the 'eyes and ears' of our law enforcement agencies."

The Civilian Radio Taxi Patrol in New York City got started in the spring of 1973 as the result of one cab driver's concern about street crime and the lack of public cooperation with the police. The program essentially consists of taxi drivers voluntarily calling police, fire, and other emergencies to their own dispatchers who, in turn, relay the information to police "hotlines" in each precinct. Of 11,780 taxis in the city, 3,000 cabs and limousines and 7,000 drivers participate. This, of course, is a big help in a city where there are 2,000 police cars and scooters with only about two-thirds of them on the street at any one time.

Liaison and guidance for the program fall under the police department's Division of Community Affairs, which believes it is one of the most valuable programs in the city and high on the priority list for continued support and expansion.

James Gillen, general manager of the Minute Men Radio Dispatch Corporation, has been the prime mover of this effort. The famous Kitty Genovese murder case in the early 1960s, where New Yorkers watched a killing and failed to respond, first aroused him. Ever since, he has wanted to get involved in some way. The use of radio-dispatched cabs to call in crimes was his idea.

Gillen started with his own association. He gained the cooperation of ten fleet owners and organized the drivers strictly on a volunteer basis. It was easier to interest drivers in this group because they have always been well organized. For example, drivers elect their own board to adjudicate disciplinary matters, and they have always emphasized customer courtesy and respect. One of their policies is to wait until passengers get safely inside their homes before pulling away. They have assisted in delivering babies, saving police officers' lives, helping elderly persons upstairs, and providing other helpful services, even though it has taken time away from their work.

**Results.** Results have been sufficiently rewarding to warrant expansion of the program. In Minute Men's first year of operation, 2,060 emergency calls were received. Each new day bring four or five more. So far emegencies have included such things as possible trouble with passengers (1,668), crime-related events (202), accidents (125), and fires (75). Now with 3,000 radio vehicles in the program citywide, the number of calls is rapidly growing. It is estimated that only about 2,000 New York City cabs have radios, but as more radios are acquired, more taxis will participate. Minute Men has 300 radio taxis, but, 1,165 of its cabs are in the program because all drivers, including those without radios, are trained to call in emergencies by using the regular 911 telephone system. Although taxis without radios cannot respond as quickly, the system is still effective.

Typical calls include such things as a person sighted on roof with a rifle, a youth riding a bicycle who is hit by an auto, hit-and-run drivers, robbery in process in a cab, a drunk in a cab, and persons in an auto stopping and robbing occupants of another auto. Response time from both police and cabbies to emergency calls has been excellent. Many times a police car is only a block away. Because there are more cabs on the street than police cars, first response may come from cab drivers themselves. In one case, a woman cabbie in Manhattan sensed trouble from two male passengers who were using foul language and had threatened sexual assault. Through the Minute Men emergency warning procedure, three cabs soon began following her and several minutes later two more squeezed in front of her. By the time she reached her destination at 95th Street, 38 taxis had protectively surrounded her. Recognizing this, her passengers excitedly left a $3 tip and hurriedly ran down a side street. The driver was safe, and the esprit de corps of the total taxi force grew. Indeed, so many cabs showed up at the scene that the police department thought there was a taxi convention in process!

It is not unusual for a dozen cabs to assist someone in trouble. When one cabbie witnessed a woman passenger being thrown out of a "gypsy" cab, he called the dispatcher. In response, one cab went to the assistance of the unconscious woman, and another gave chase. In a short while, as many as a dozen cabs participated in the pursuit. As a consequence, the driver of the "gypsy" cab was apprehended some 20 minutes later by police who had been informed by taxi radio.

In another case, a cab driver tailed a bank robber, ending up pursuing him on foot until the criminal was captured by police. In still another incident, a cabbie cornered a gunman engaged in a shooting spree and eventually assisted in his apprehension. Gerard Meister, an owner and director of public affairs for Minute Men, says that the lives of two housing police officers were saved by drivers in this program. Although there are numerous interesting examples, many of the day-by-day, unpublicized emergencies have turned out to be just as important.

**Operations and Training.** Training is necessary to engender confidence and motivation. Although not lengthy, it serves the purpose and is provided by both police and taxi cab personnel. Minute Men has training courses every week for new drivers. It includes two hours in radio operation and one hour in police and emergency techniques. Drivers are instructed to observe and report, but not to get physically involved in incidents. They are taught how to report street crimes, suspicious acts, fires, accidents, and unusual occurrences, with emphasis on proper descriptions and locations. Detailed forms are used to make it more convenient to describe persons and vehicles in a comprehensive way.

Drivers are trained to use special procedures for emergencies which occur inside the cab. Cab owners believe these simple procedures are almost as effective as another, more expensive nonvoice system.

The more costly, computerized system is called the Voice-PLUS digitalized message, which at the push of a button identifies whether the driver is on call, off duty, in an emergency, or engaged in anywhere up to 99 different coded activities. All voice and coded messages are visually seen and also permanently recorded on a hard-copy printout at the base station. The dispatcher can interrogate any car in the system, whether occupied or not, to determine its status. But at a cost of $200 per cab plus central installation expenses, fleet owners have been reluctant to install the full system.

The special noncomputerized procedures do not require additional costs. In regular operation, the procedure upon accepting a customer is to call the dispatcher, give the cab number, and wait for a response from the dispatcher before giving a destination. However, when in trouble, the driver is instructed to call in and give his number and destination without being acknowledged, thus breaking radio procedure. Anytime regular radio procedure is broken, the dispatcher automatically knows that the driver is in difficulty. With recognition of an emergency, the dispatcher simply holds other calls. He then asks the driver, "Is this yellow cab number so and so?" The driver answers "yes" and disconnects. Although there is nothing suspicious about this procedure, the word *yellow* verifies an emergency in process; otherwise, *yellow* is omitted. The dispatcher then calls the police hotline and also notifies other cabs in the vicinity to follow or meet the cab at the announced destination.

Participants in radio patrol use special identification cards signed by a police official. Large decals also appear on the sides of cabs reading, "In Cooperation with New York City Police Department — Minute Men Taxi Patrol." It is impressive to see cabs roving about with their bright decals, indicative of close cooperation with police and willingness to assist anyone who stops them — a considerably different attitude from the recent past when most of the public seemed to turn away from anything that looked like trouble.

As a result of this program, innovations have taken place. Some drivers now voluntarily ride sections of the city in their off-duty hours, patrolling high-crime areas and shopping districts. Usually two taxis at a time patrol several blocks in one-hour shifts. Other private firms, which use radio dispatched automobiles and trucks (such as security companies and hauling businesses), are joining the emergency call system. Also most of the private radio limousines are now in the program.

**Program Costs.** So far, costs have been minimal. The biggest expense has been for radios, which have averaged over $1,000 each plus the cost of the central equipment. For vehicles with radios, it is a simple matter to put them into the system by using existing dispatchers and frequency equipment. In the case of Minute Men the owners contributed $61,000 for an additional frequency to be used for emergencies only. Other taxi fleets could use this same frequency, but they would have to install their own base stations at approximately $3,000 each and pay a monthly rental of $125. Installation of a special $40 frequency crystal is also needed for each cab.

As yet, it has not been necessary to add dispatchers to meet the slight increase in the volume of calls. However, as more and more cabs are added to the system, extra dispatchers could become necessary on some shifts. The police department could expedite some calls by channeling them directly to the police communications switchboard. This would be cumbersome, however, because taxis travel citywide while each police communication board functions at the precinct level. The logistics could be worked out. Presently there are no police department plans to alter their system or to help finance base stations or radios for private use.

Minute Men point out that one way to sustain some costs is to charge membership dues to drivers for participation in the crime prevention program. Jim Gillen believes that as little as 50¢ per month dues could do two things: (1) increase driver interest, and (2) help pay for identification cards, decals, newsletters, and other minor items.

Some private businesses have made contributions. For program promotion and information purposes, the First National City Bank, in conjunction with the New York City Police Foundation, paid for decals and for the publication of 10,000 pamphlets entitled *Civilian Radio Taxi Patrol.*

On a much broader scale, Minute Men would like to carry their idea nationwide, start a semiannual awards system for outstanding member performance, print a monthly newsletter, and hire an experienced person to train drivers and motivate fleet owners in other cities. But the funds for this are not yet available.

**Conclusion.** This public-spirited program could spread to many other cities in the United States. Minute Men already reports some 50 or more inquiries. Success will depend largely on the leadership and motivation of local taxi association members and the cooperation they get from police departments in each jurisdiction. The reasons Minute Men is effective and responds to a higher percentage of emergency calls than many other radio patrol groups are because of its more formal and viable structure, excellent training program, and the genuine concern of its leaders. Haphazard operations have produced more limited results.


## Uniformed and Paid Civilians

As we have already stated, this is not a review of patrol units integrated within the formal structure of the police department or directly supervised by them, such as community service officers or career-oriented employees. However, there are at least two concepts worth assessing which are on the borderline of our consideration and, where necessary, can fill the gap between sworn officers and volunteers. Particularly in seriously understaffed departments, part-time paid civilians and uniformed auxiliary police can be valuable additions to almost any department and can help to increase effectiveness substantially without overly burdensome expenditures. Two of these programs serve as good examples.


### Police and Citizens Together against Crime –
### Rochester, New York

**Objectives.** Police and Citizens Together against Crime (PACTAC) uses citizens as partners with police in two-person teams to patrol regular beats on foot and bicycle. It started in April 1973 with 40 civilian and 40 police officers. Now twelve teams of two persons each work in the high-crime areas, half on the east and half on the west sides of this city of 300,000 persons and 39 square miles. In brief, it has been an experiment in the value of redeeming the foot patrol as an operational feature of urban police work and of employing civilians as police paraprofessionals.

There are several program objectives: (1) to improve police-community relations, (2) to deter street crime, and (3) to find a productive and feasible division of labor between police and paraprofessionals. The program has helped police officers develop closer ties with community residents and a keener appreciation of the life-styles and values of the city's different communities. The paraprofessionals have served as liaison between the police and neighborhood institutions and improved communication links.

**Operations.** PACTAC is administered as an experimental program by the Planning and Research Division of the police department. The program provides extra police patrols, especially during high-crime periods, by paying regular officers overtime and PACTAC civilians $4 per hour. The work schedule is four-hour shifts, 2 or 3 days per week. Police have to volunteer for the program in order to participate; they usually do so because they either want the freedom of walking a beat or enjoy communicating directly with citizens. However, for many, the overtime pay is the most important element.

Since the program is communication-oriented, older persons have proved as effective as the young, and in some cases even more so. The living in the area where one works is a requirement which makes it easier for PACTAC workers to get to know more residents and increases success in dealing with loiterers and potential troublemakers due to the more personalized contact. The minimum age limit is 18 years old, and several seniors are over 60 years of age. Civilians do not carry weapons (not even clubs); however, they do operate two-way radios and, before assignment, receive 24 class hours of training at the Police Academy plus field work. There are no shortages for PACTAC civilian candidates because of the wide publicity. The number of male and female workers is split about evenly.

PACTAC provides police with the opportunity to be seen in many neighborhoods and on foot, important psychological factors for residents. Moreover, the use of bicycles provides sufficient mobility without the restrictions and confinement experienced in patrol cars. Bicycles are pushed or parked during conversation with merchants and residents.

**Results.** The police department considers the program moderately successful. Although there is little statistical evidence of crime reduction, officials believe the additional street patrols have been a deterrent to crime. "Some good criminal apprehensions have been made also," say Lieutenant Thomas L. Conway, in charge of the experiment.

Cost benefit and community relation aspects have been valuable. Although they are less skilled, additional and valuable workers have been made available at reasonable cost. Overtime pay to regular officers has provided fully trained, extra persons to patrol during high-crime periods at a cost lower than that of simply adding new officers. Public relations benefits have varied from one community to another depending not only on demographic and social characteristics but also on the style and ability of each team leader. Moreover, the police department states that the program developed enthusiasm in police officers about the value of foot patrols and created a more responsive attitude toward residents, both of which have made police work less difficult for officers in the PACTAC areas.

**Lessons.** A number of valuable lessons have been learned:

1. Teams were made more productive by making them more mobile. The combination of walking, bicycling, and autos was found most effective.
2. Civilians performed better when given fixed responsibilities, clearly defined and carefully taught. Civilian experience was minimal, making regular officers uncomfortable and some disinterested in team work.

3. Greater administrative flexibility was found necessary. Some teams needed to be moved to more active areas and to work nights.
4. Information sharing was too limited between PACTAC and regular patrols.
5. Greater team stability was found necessary. It was also demonstrated that sworn officers appeared more concerned and responsive when working with civilians.

**Community Service Officers versus PACTAC.** In addition to PACTAC personnel, seven paraprofessional Community Service Officers (CSOs) perform some duties which are similar in nature to those of PACTAC. Recruitment is stricter for CSOs than for PACTAC. They are selected because of their potential to make good police officers and to progress upward on the career ladder. Those not qualified to be police officers will be phased out; others may go into cadet training school, and still others may be requested to pursue further education or obtain high school diplomas where necessary.

Duties consist of service-type calls, which ordinarily consume about 80 percent of regular police work. They are uniformed and drive police cars marked as Community Service vehicles. They are additional eyes and ears for the police department and do not directly respond to criminal-type complaints. For example, they follow up on barking dog complaints, noise problems, illegal use of fire hydrants for recreation, etc. In many cases, they have been found to be more successful than police in dealing with youth groups and residents because of their less threatening nature.

This more neutral role of the Community Service Officer is almost identical to PACTAC paraprofessionals, believed to be more effective in performing duties in the nonenforcement role. In both the PACTAC and CSO program, communication with residents has remained at a high level, and the police department has benefited from this additional link to the community. Where some community groups had complained of poor police performance, many now applaud the department because they see police, CSOs, and PACTAC civilians as a comprehensive force, integrated and more responsive.

Some police officials view the CSO program as more lasting and possibly more effective than PACTAC over the long run. Permanency and the ability of CSOs to release police from large quantities of routine work are attributes PACTAC lacks so far. Presently, PACTAC is limited in its patrol functions. On the other hand, PACTAC is more flexible in its selection of personnel and offers another range in age and style of operation for civilians.

*Auxiliary Police in New York City*

The second example is the auxiliary police, who perform much of the same kind of tasks as PACTAC or other paid civilian safety officers but who, themselves, are usually never compensated except for the provision of uniforms, equipment, and certain expenses.

**Largest Civilian Police Force in World.** New York City's Auxiliary Police is in this category — a voluntary organization of citizens who wear regular police uniforms and help perform many police duties. They are not paid and do not carry weapons, with the exception of a few who are specially licensed to do so. Their power of arrest is no greater than that of a regular citizen, except in specially declared emergencies. Quasi-military and well trained, they have an excellent record of personal safety.

The force was established 24 years ago as an adjunct to the police department in case of civil defense emergencies and natural disasters — a requirement of the State Defense Emergency Act for all cities in New York. But its role expanded naturally to meet the city's rising crime rate and was meshed with regular police operations and placed directly under the responsibility of the police department in 1967. The 5,000 members constitute the largest civilian police force in the world.

The Auxiliary Police provides its members the opportunity to study police work, learn police goals and objectives, and assist regular police officers. Two of the organization's goals are (1) the establishing of mutual respect between police and citizens, and (2) the creation of an atmosphere conducive to greater public cooperation and police effectiveness. The group has come a long way in reaching these goals. The Auxiliary Police force's focus is now on neighborhood crime prevention.

"The best form of crime prevention and detection," stated a former commander of the New York City Police Auxiliary Forces Section, Captain Ronald P. Brosen, "is men in police uniforms who patrol an area they know, and among people they know. Those who work with us are trained, screened and supervised by the police department."

**Recruitment and Training.** Qualifications for the auxiliary force are almost as strict as those for regular police officers. Good reputation and character and no convictions for felonies or serious misdemeanors are prime prerequisites. Fluent command of the English language is necessary, and serious physical, mental, or nervous conditions are not permitted. Medical examinations are options of the department, but full background investigations, fingerprints, and a loyalty oath are mandatory. Applicants must be residents of New York City and male or female American citizens (or declared intentions of becoming a citizen) between the ages of 21 and 55 years. Volunteers 17 to 21 years of age may be enrolled as auxiliary trainees, and there are some age exceptions for persons over 55 who possess special skills.

Recruits must attend a Primary Training School within their own borough. Some of the courses include criminal law, police procedures, Auxiliary Police duties, unarmed self-defense, narcotics enforcement, emergency procedures, and other related matters. Training continues on the job, and intermediate and advanced courses are made available for those who want to seek promotion later. The ranks for promotion in the volunteer service are inspector (commanding officer), deputy inspector (executive officer), captain, lieutenant, sergeant, patrolman/woman, and trainee.

A Board of Review, composed of the commanding officer of the Auxiliary Forces Section as chairperson and superior officers of the regular police department and the Auxiliary Police, decide matters of promotion, awards, and discipline.

Turnover has been about 13 percent but is improving because of an increased "esprit de corps," uniform allowance, and improved relations with regular police officers. Although some police still resent volunteers "interfering" in their work and have been slow to come to the assistance of auxiliaries, Commissioner Michael Codd has called for a massive publicity campaign to attract as many qualified volunteers as possible to the department. Of those who apply, only about 60 percent actually complete training and are assigned to duty.

There are a number of valid reasons for which citizens join special police forces. The real reason people join the auxiliary, says Martin A. Greenberg, president of the Auxiliary Police Benevolent Association, is that they want to meet people and gain a sense of security. "Volunteer efforts tend not to last unless they are based on social contacts," says one officer. Many volunteers, of course, join because they were not eligible for the regular force. But many join because their motivations are high and they want to do something for the community. In 1973, a total of 673 left the program for the following reasons: resignations, 142; dropped for inactivity, 343; dismissed for cause, 180; and death, 8.

**Organization.** Auxiliary Police are under the direction of the commanding officer of the Police Department's Auxiliary Forces Section. They have units at all levels of operation — citwide, borough, division, precinct, and park areas. Park patrol units may use police motorcycles or private vehicles. There is a taxi task force unit and also a special task force for recruitment, headquarters security, and administration.

Headquarters is divided as follows:

1. Headquarters staff
2. Investigation
3. Communication
4. Education lectures
5. Public relations
6. Recruitment and retention
7. Women's unit

A patrol precinct has an auxiliary commanding officer, executive officer, and personnel officer. Usually one auxiliary sergeant supervises five to ten persons. An additional sergeant and lieutenant are added for units with eleven to nineteen persons.

**Duties.** The primary responsibility of the Auxiliary Police is to assist the police department in emergencies, but in actuality, most of their time is devoted to crime prevention and the important role of additional eyes and ears for the police.

The force is divided into two sections: emergency and patrol. Those who choose emergency duty receive vigorous training in the use of tools, specialized equipment, and first-aid and rescue techniques. Those in patrol are equipped with walkie-talkies and are selected from the same neighborhood where they live. They work in pairs at assigned posts, such as bus stops, houses of worship, playgrounds, and shopping areas. All volunteers may be called to assist regular police in crowd control for civic events, elections, parades, and also in emergencies, such as missing children, blackouts, bad weather, etc.

Patrol duties are carefully supervised. In no case can volunteers patrol alone. But they can patrol in a variety of teams: two men may patrol together, one woman and two men, trainees with at least two men, and volunteers along with a regular patrol officer. Patrol must be done in the regulation blue uniform and identification shield. Importantly, volunteers may not relieve police from their regular patrol duties because this would lend to conflict with union and employment regulations and understandings.

A normal tour of active duty for volunteers is 4 hours, but this can be extended in certain cases. Volunteers are not assigned to plain-clothes duty, crime investigation, strikes, hazardous duty, or civil rights demonstrations. They are also not assigned between the hours of 1:00 A.M. and 8:00 A.M. The city pays for uniforms, equipment, and maintenance, and transportation costs are reimbursed.

Proper written communication is stressed. Each volunteer makes use of an Auxiliary Police Response Report for reporting hours and emergencies. Log books are carefully maintained, and those on duty must obtain permission if they desire to be relieved from a tour of duty.

There are numerous specific duties. Auxiliary Police may be assigned to assist the Neighborhood Police Team sergeant or as aides to the precinct officer to assist in operations, administration, planning, community affairs, training, election duty, telephone switchboard, station house security, receptionist, and clerical responsibilities. A citywide mounted unit is also being formed. Other duties include the techniques of area situation, vertical patrol, and assignment with tactical patrol teams.

**Conclusion.** There appears to be little question that the mere presence of the Auxiliary Police has helped to maintain order in many areas and deter assailants and burglars. The 60,000 hours per month (up from 26,000 hours a few years ago) of extra service to the police department is a significant contribution — a program the police department needs and does not wish to lose. Nevertheless, there are volunteers who do not wish to wear uniforms or be engaged in semi-military-style operations. Even some police wish to discourage civilians from patroling in uniform and endangering themselves. It is because of these diversities of how citizens want to participate that more flexible and freer institutions have also developed, such as private block associations and mobile patrols more integrated in the community. There appears to be room and need for a variety of methods.

# 6　Police-Community Councils

## Background

A police officer's first impression at the mention of police-community councils is usually some kind of police review board to investigate police wrongdoing or citizen complaints against the police. This is not the kind of community board discussed in this chapter. We are concerned with citizen committees beneficial to law enforcement officers and the community, which are are set up to assist police and resolve neighborhood issues. These citizen bodies can fulfill these objectives more effectively by dealing primarily with issues of crime prevention and not incurring the hostility of police over perhaps serious but isolated incidents. Formal police investigations are probably better handled by bodies specifically set up for that purpose.

The focus on citizen councils here is to prevent crime and to inform and motivate citizens. Neighborhood councils in this context are used to assess and relay information about the formation of block associations, home and street security, city services, and special neighborhood problems. Some have gotten involved in policy decisions on such things as traffic, police assignments, response time, and other issues. On the whole, these have been constructive contributions to the police and have improved overall relationships between police and citizens. However, some neighborhood committees have seriously deteriorated because of such factors as lack of resources, poor leadership from the heads of certain police divisions, ill-informed lower-echelon police officers, and a misunderstanding of the value of neighborhood crime prevention committees.

Although not all citizen committees have been productive in all cities, most police departments continually strive to improve the quality of these committees and especially maintain those which have proved viable and have made significant contributions. The failure of some should not lead to the abandonment of an entire program.

In another example discussed here, police have developed a mechanism for citizens to sit down with officers in various task forces and help to create basic police policy. Not only has the project gotten citizens deeply involved, but it has opened doors for the rank-and-file police officers to express their opinions and help set policy. As such, the city has been able to develop more permanent crime prevention techniques and avoid potential police incidents.

## Objectives

Police-community councils are valuable to both police and residents. They should be established to assess local crime problems, to plan with police, and to recommend solutions. To be acceptable to the police and successful in reaching specific objectives, it must be made clear that they are not "watchdogs" over police performance or a review committee for complaints against the police. The objectives should revolve primarily around crime prevention, working out policies with police as partners, creating and maintaining block clubs and other crime-fighting groups, developing effective communication links between residents and police, and pursuing other matters which can assist police and improve the neighborhood.

## Membership

Membership should consist of neighborhood leaders, block captains, and other categories of residents. The board of a block association federation or a committee of block captains could also function as the district police-community council, but duplication should be avoided.

Police and city officials should participate in member selection, but residents themselves should be entitled to appoint the majority of membership. A serious mistake made by many communities has been to allow police officials to appoint the full membership, thereby scuttling the idea of genuine citizen participation. Citizens should be involved from the beginning of the program.

## Organizational Steps

In organizing a police-community council, the following steps are recommended:

1. *Outside assistance.* Retain some inexpensive outside assistance from the university, business groups, League of Women Voters, Urban League, or other civic bodies. Graduate students can be used to send notices, call meetings and work out agendas, keep records, and interview both police and residents about what ought to be accomplished. The city should provide funds for pamphlets, newsletters, and other expenses.

2. *List of priorities.* From interviews, case histories, and other records, a list of policy areas can be constructed and priority discussions and workshops set. Full and accurate reports and statistics must be provided by the police department. Only confidential material should be withheld.

3. *Role of patrol officer.* Beat patrol officers as well as other police and city officials should sit in on committee meetings. At all times it is necessary

to capture the "street wisdom" of the beat patrol officers and incorporate their ideas into policy changes and improvement in neighborhood-level duty. Patrol officers particularly have been very pleased with this approach for it has given them a realistic opportunity to get their message to top officials.

4. *Written results.* Policy ideas, suggested changes, and other concepts should be put in writing and passed to the chief of police who, in turn, should be required to respond to each request of the committee. Lack of response is the surest way to kill committee effectiveness.

5. *Distribution.* New policies and concepts should be distributed widely to all police officers and police civilians, civilian members of committees city-wide, news media, and other interested parties.

6. *City endorsement.* This entire process plus the structural arrangement of the committees should be officially endorsed by the mayor and city council, preferably by city ordinance. Importantly, the chief of police should incorporate related rules and regulations into required police procedures, manuals, and training programs.

7. *Awards.* Officials should issue certificates of appreciation to deserving committees, outstanding service awards to certain members and police officers, and unit excellence awards to effective police teams.

8. *Expansion.* Success and experience for a few councils should be gained before expanding to other areas. Too rapid a rate of growth could destroy the entire program. It is important to stress that any inappropriate political or vigilante activity from one or two councils should not be reason enough to disband other councils.

9. *Central committee.* In some communities, a citywide committee — representing the neighborhood councils — may be useful. Some communities have even found this committee a good resource through which to pass on complaints against police. There is usually less police apprehension about a basic crime prevention group; in fact, some police departments support this idea. The major role of this central committee would be to review citywide police policies, coordinate neighborhood council activities, promote citywide block club organization, and engage in the whole field of crime prevention.

**Police Policy Bureau — Dayton, Ohio**

*Objectives and Duties*

One of the best examples of police-citizen cooperation is the Police Policy Bureau of Dayton, Ohio. Skeptics said it would never work and that no meaningful policy would ever come out of it. Yet local officials call it successful.

Headed by two seasoned police officers, the Bureau reports directly to the chief of police and combines the efforts of a cross section of Dayton residents: paid and unpaid civilians (adults and youths). The sworn officers have responsibility in the following areas:

1. To maintain communication with the street officers by riding with them periodically
2. To visit various community groups and schools to invite participation in the program
3. To assist in identifying areas in need of policy definition
4. To critique policy drafts in an effort to improve the organization and readability of the drafts
5. To maintain contact with the Command Staff to ensure that their suggestions and comments are understood and considered by the Bureau
6. To assist the project assistants in collecting information and developing a full picture of the areas of enforcement they will be dealing with in task forces[a]

The officers are assisted by paid graduate students from local universities who serve as resource and administrative staff for a series of citizen task forces. Students are used as committee aides because they have been found to be less intimidating and more acceptable to civilians who have little law enforcement expertise and are more easily subdued by experienced police officers. Task forces are composed of street-level officers and residents of each neighborhood. Civilians are selected on the basis of political neutrality, interest in the future of Dayton, and representativeness of the neighborhoods from which they come.

Each task force studies one selected police problem. According to Sergeant J.R. Hopkins, coordinator of the Bureau, the procedure is as follows: "It [task force], through close liaison with officers in the field, is continuously attempting to predict possible problem areas and then calmly address them without the spector of a citizen complaint waiting to be satisfied. Once a problem area has been identified, police officers and citizens are placed in a task force with a project assistant [graduate student] as recorder and facilitator. The police officer furnishes input as to what is currently happening at street level; the citizen furnishes his viewpoint as to how this is accepted, and the project assistant records and, where necessary, researches for the task force. The end result of this exchange is a policy draft." The draft is then passed along to the police chief, who may accept, modify, or reject it.

The Bureau's philosophy is described by Hopkins:

The philosophy of our process is to attempt to capture the "street wisdom" of experienced officers, mostly patrolmen, and reduce it to writing for

---

[a]*Citizen and Officer Policy Making System,* Dayton Policy Making Staff, Dayton, Ohio, Police Department, 1974.

edification of those officers to follow. We in the police profession understand that officers use discretion during every hour they are on duty, and the administration gives tacit approval to these discretionary responses. However, when use of discretion creates upheaval in the status quo, through a citizen's complaint, that same administration is quick to "Monday Morning Quarterback" the officer's actions. Officers who are caught in this type situation usually have no way to justify their actions or to defend themselves when departmental charges result. This predicament is created because most departments do not supply their officers with guidelines beyond that which is written into the laws or *ordinances they are responsible for enforcing. The standard reaction is* for command to immediately issue an order, drafted solely to assure that problem does not occur again. An order written in this "stop gap" fashion is usually extremely narrow and many times fails to respond to anything beyond the exact same problem. People involved in police operations are acutely aware that the same problem never presents itself in the exact same manner a second time. Consequently, orders developed in this manner soon prove to be practically worthless.

Patricia Hamblatt, a graduate assistant for the project, confirms Officer Hopkins's description:

A lot of what an officer does is discretionary — outside the realm of the *rules*, but both legal and effective. The idea behind the Policy Bureau was that for years police department policy was made without this street input — made in an ivory tower. People out on the front lines had no input as to what they did, as to how they had survived out in the street for, say 25 years, whereas those inside making policy may not have been on the street for 10 to 15 years. So, they decided to let the front line officers have more voice. And since citizens are the recipients of services, they felt it was also necessary to have their input — important to hear what types and kinds and levels of service the citizen wanted.

Implementation of this philosophy was designed to lead to acceptable procedures of operation under many varying circumstances.

*Methodology*

There are six stages in the development of task force product:

1. Research and investigation into the elements of the project began first by project assistants reviewing the department's procedures manual. Working in conjunction with officers in the department, they developed a list of policy areas which needed action. Then command and street police personnel were asked to list in order of priority those areas which they felt were in need of policy definition. Special requests from officers and citizens have also been sources for policy review.

2. Stage two is the presentation of a narrative. Once a topic is chosen in the first stage, project assistants work up a presentation of basic information

regarding the policy problem under examination. This is done after consultation with Dayton police officers. The narrative which is generated accompanies a set of questions which probe citizen response to problems associated with the policy topic.

3. Stage three involves the selection of prospective task force members from those who respond to the questionnaire. Initially the chief of police and a council of command officers were to play a role in this function, but the current procedure is different, involving a review by the graduate assistants and officers assigned to the Bureau. Officer selection is part of this stage, progressing simultaneously with the search for citizen members. The Bureau selects officers for each task force who have some expertise in that area of law enforcement.

4. Stage four is the actual conduct of task forces. One project assistant is assigned to each group, and it is his or her responsibility to lead the group through a coherent and comprehensive review of all the facets of the topic to be addressed. Once the group feels it has adequately addressed and resolved each point, the project assistant organizes the information that the group feels should be included in a policy statement on the topic. Each task force meets nearly every week, usually from ½ hour to 2 hours. The task forces continue for several months, totaling up to 20 hours of formal meetings. The assistants take part of the time to acquaint the citizens with police department systems and with the policy problem in question. Students serve as discussion leaders, recording the results and drafting policy from them. Outside experts are also brought in as resources for the meetings.

5. Stage five involves the distribution of the task force's final draft to all commands within the department. All personnel are invited to critique the work within 10 days. The crucial review by the police chief and his/her council occurs at this time too. The chief of police is advised by the council about the acceptability of the policy draft and any comments, corrections, or suggestions concerning substantive or technical issues. The entire task force may attend this meeting and defend, if necessary, any facet of the policy that falls under attack. The police chief then gives final direction on what should be done about the task force recommendations.

6. The sixth and final stage is the distribution of the approved policy to all police personnel. The Bureau staff reports:

We have felt it imperative that each man be given a copy of each policy so that he may familiarize himself with its contents. To further facilitate the officers' review of the material, we are attempting to summarize each policy and place it into what we have called our Field Officer's Guide — a small manual that the officer can carry with him and use as a reference. If he wishes more information on a given topic, he is to refer to his Manual of Procedure in which he has the complete policy statements.

So far policies have been developed for family disputes, response to the mentally ill, vehicle inventory, field interview, and traffic. Policies are now being developed for curfew, shoplifting, public nuisances, probation violation, school disturbances, and rape. Other topics are being considered.

## Conclusion

Unrelenting efforts have been made to ensure that the task force recommendations conform to the real world — on the street where the police officers do their work. Those associated with the Police Policy Bureau, both civilian and police, concur that this has been done. Moreover, relationships have gradually improved between police officers and civilians to the point where suspicions about this being another do-nothing program or a police review board are almost nonexistent. It has also opened a new channel of communication for officers in the lower echelons with those at the command level. Indeed, one of the principal reasons for the program's success is that the rank-and-file officer has been given greater influence in policy making.

## Precinct Community Councils — New York City

New York City has had police-community councils starting as far back as the 1930s. They were called Coordination Councils then. But councils have a habit of coming into and going out of existence or being active or inactive depending upon the urgency of the times. This has meant that purposes and structure have changed over the years.

The present structure was created in the 1950s, one which is youth-oriented and concerned with problems of delinquency. But as crime increased dramatically in all categories, community councils began to deal with all phases of both adult and juvenile crimes, and the program's name was changed to Precinct Community Councils in 1966. In some precincts, separate youth councils also function.

## Organization

Each of the city's 73 precincts has a precinct community council. To get the program started, in each area board members were selected by the police department until elections could be held. Six executive officers for each board are elected annually from the general membership who attend the election. New nominees are selected at membership meetings two months prior to the general election, and nominations are also permitted from the floor on election day. Anywhere from 50 to 200 persons have shown up for elections. The general rule is that one needs only to attend three meetings to be eligible to vote and that anyone from the neighborhood can become a member of the council, although most members turn out to be representatives of civic organizations in the area.

Councils have been meeting faithfully for the past 10 years. Monthly meetings draw anywhere from 20 to 80 people and sometimes as many as 200 when a special issue arises.

Each police precinct captain is an ex officio member of that area's council, and the precinct captain or one of his/her assistants attends each meeting. They help guide council activity and encourage resident attendance. The department emphasizes that the precinct commander would be very reluctant to call a meeting of residents without involving the area's police-community council. Where police teams operate, the team sergeant and one or two of his/her co-workers attend the monthly meetings, which are held in different sections of the community in order to involve as many people as possible. The police help set meeting agenda and develop meeting notices and other literature. Besides the limited resources assigned from the regular police budget, councils have no funds of their own.

*Responsibilities and Duties*

Although various community matters are discussed, councils are advisory and their interests are primarily crime-oriented. Nevertheless, some councils spend over half of their time on noncrime issues, such as consumer affairs, community development, city services, etc.

On the whole, council sessions have been constructive and informative, and only occasionally have agitators attended meetings. So far voting has been noncontroversial. "We would be shocked if there was any opposition," says Chairwoman Shirley Moore of the 113th Precinct Community Council (Jamaica area), reflecting the common purpose and understanding of the membership.

In its literature, the police department states that the councils should "strive to develop an understanding of police objectives and gain a recognition of the citizen's responsibility in maintaining the peace." The department hopes to gain more responsive police attitudes and better awareness of the community's point of view. It has already been demonstrated that liaison and communication between the police and community have improved through the use of community councils.

Relations have improved so much in some communities that community council members are given wide access to the police precinct stations and are even provided with keys to the crime prevention rooms so that typewriters and other office equipment can be used. There are cordial greetings between the police and citizens now. This is in sharp contrast to the situation just a few years ago when police and residents were barely talking to each other.

## Effectiveness

In almost any city or county with numerous units of citizen bodies and other service groups, one will find that some groups function well and others do not. In New York City, police officials estimate that less than half of the precinct councils can be rated highly successful, most are mediocre, and a significant percentage are not at all effective. According to police officials, some 15 or 20 councils are very effective, making the whole investment worthwhile. They believe that resident disinterest in some areas should not be a factor against community council development elsewhere. Each community should seek its own level of resident participation and effectiveness and quality-of-life standards. Failure elsewhere should not be discouraging, but rather teach lessons of how to succeed. The councils which are successful are the ones worth following.

## The Future

The future of police-community councils in New York City depends on a number of factors. Perhaps most important is the police department's interest, which appears to be high at this time. In this regard, Roosevelt Dunning, Deputy Commissioner of Community Affairs (where responsibility for community councils falls), has appointed a task force and staff to assess and strengthen the program and develop a model to follow. The department would like to see each council incorporate and develop its own constitution and operational procedures. Police officials are now requesting greater resources and city support for the councils.

## Operation Get Involved — Dallas, Texas

Another experience is a series of beat committees in Dallas which have helped set some policies but have been mostly used for crime prevention purposes.

*Operation Get Involved* (OGI) was initiated in February 1970, by Dallas' former Chief of Police, Frank Dyson, to build citizen rapport and assistance to police through crime-fighting committees at the beat level. Any adult resident of the beat or one who owned property there was eligible for membership. During the past several years, out of 111 police beats over 50 beat committees functioned, some rather effectively and others less than satisfactorily. At this stage, the program is being phased into a more independent citizen organization.

Police officers and city officials who are intimately familiar with the program praise its value. Others are considerably more negative because of several reasons: (1) poor resident attendance at meetings, (2) fear of "super-patriot" types who dominate some committees, and (3) the controversial involvement of a few committees in politics.

In Octber 1974, the program was abruptly dropped as an official city effort; on the other hand, many of the committees continue to function because residents in these areas believe the program is valuable. Local chambers of commerce as well as other citizen groups continue to develop committees; for them, there is a new feeling of excitement about long-term success.

Dallas is a large city and, like most urban areas, is short of police. Of the population of 1,327,321, 17.4 percent belong to minority groups. Of its 2,000-member police force, 950 are in the Patrol Division. An average of seven officers are assigned to a beat, representing an area of about 5,000 persons.

In the past, experience showed that it was easier to organize beat committees in the middle-income groups and with middle-aged and elderly persons. The young did not seem to want to get involved. Indeed, both low- and high-income populations have lacked enthusiasm or confidence, so that resident involvement would not make much of a difference. The black population is particularly difficult to convince. Therefore, the city has been concentrating its organizational efforts in the high crime areas where citizens are most concerned.

*Organization*

Organizational structure has always been a problem. The program has bounced back and forth between the Community Services and Patrol Divisions twice and has had three different directors since its inception. Directors were assigned without much consideration of whether they supported the concept; therefore, the program ran into difficulties at times lacked the necessary effective leadership. This lack of leadership from the top has made it difficult for the rank-and-file police officer to accept it.

Community Services has been enthusiastic, while Patrol has been less than enchanted with the program; nevertheless, there is general agreement that it ought to be located under Patrol. But without the understanding, care, and personal involvement of regular beat patrol officers, Operation Get Involved has suffered. Support from the Patrol Division was an essential ingredient that was lacking most of the time.

The program never had a budget of its own. Resources were allocated from either the Community Services or Patrol budgets. Regular officers were assigned to the project, usually three to a beat. As the project progressed, one officer from each beat was designated coordinator and received overtime pay to attend meetings and perform related duties. Nevertheless, even overtime pay was not enough to entice some officers to this duty. Yet in the beginning, although the majority of officers expressed little understanding of or concern for the program, the percentage who cared reversed as officers recognized the value of community involvement and how much it could help the police officer's job.

**First Phase.** In the first phase, a sergeant and five patrol officers from Community Services were given citywide responsibilities. Their jobs were to identify community leaders and help organize committees. Contacts were made through such organizations as the Chamber of Commerce, Kiwanis, Rotary, Lions, Community Action Agency, Parent-Teachers Associations, apartment management groups, churches, banks, insurance companies, and others. Through these organizations, the media, and brochures, residents joined. The police department selected committee chairpersons. The structure was rigid and controlled and was directed centrally by the department.

**Second Phase.** In order to gain more citizen participation and sustenance, police and residents agreed that the committees needed more self-reliance and purpose. In the second phase, committees were encouraged to develop constitutions, by-laws, and methods for electing officers and board members. Consequently, each board elected its own chairperson, vice-chairperson, and secretary, but committee structures remained the same. The most active subcommittees were crime review, youth, and membership.

In addition to beat committees, there were division committees composed of beat representatives from larger areas. Five division committees met periodically with the Patrol Division commanders. Typical subcommittees of the division committees were public relations, traffic, membership, program, crime activity, neighborhood improvement, and street lighting.

Finally, an executive committee, composed of one member elected from each of the five division committees, met monthly, in an advisory capacity, with the chief of police to discuss policies, citywide strategies, and other executive matters. The main criticisms about both the division and the executive committees were that they met too infrequently and they did not make as much impact on policy and performance as officials had hoped.

To encourage committee attendance and better leadership, an incentive awards program based on an accumulative point system was set up. Certificates of appreciation were awarded to individual members, outstanding service awards to beat leaders, and unit excellence awards to successful beat committees. Also, procedure manuals, films, and various literature were used as training devices for beat chairpersons.

The three beat officers on each beat worked closely with committee and subcommittee chairpersons. The second watch officer acted as the coordinator who kept committees informed about the types of crime most prevalent in the area, trends, criminal operations, crime prevention techniques, wanted persons, and license number of stolen vehicles.

**Third Phase.** In the present and third organizational phase of Operation Get Involved, widespread community participation and more specific crime solutions are being emphasized. The police hardware and community relations phases are over, according to Eugene Denton, assistant city manager. Crime suppression, greater police presence, computers, and hardware have not had much effect on crime here. Better police training, greater understanding, and broad-based citizen support are now recognized as the most vital crime prevention ingredients.

Such things as target hardening, "stake-outs," reward systems, family crisis training, and methods to reduce assaults and rapes are elements of this new phase. "Police now recognize the importance of dealing with citizens," says Denton. And according to local officials, a passive Operation Get Involved, or whatever remains of it, will have to find new methods and support to survive and prove its value.

*Objectives and Duties*

The basic objectives of Operation Get Involved — at least for the beat committees still in the program — are to reduce and prevent crime through joint police-community cooperation and to improve police-resident relations through better communications. The program enables police to become more aware of what the community expects and allows residents to understand police problems. It is designed to make people feel included and police more responsive. Citizens are encouraged to report crimes and unusual circumstances, and police are motivated to respond more quickly and effectively. The end product is a police-citizen partnership.

Beat committee meetings cover many topics. Agenda are kept short so that in-depth discussions can be held on important issues, with crime prevention being only one of them. Much time is devoted to neighborhood improvement, health, clean-up, and better city services; also, neighborhood crime statistics are analyzed regularly. Specific crimes, crime incident maps, bicycle-marking projects, rooftop and alley numbering, information on target hardening, better locks, helicopter use, polygraph techniques, use of dogs, and police procedures are some of the subjects and projects either discussed or implemented. During the latter months of the full OGI program, it was a problem finding different and interesting speakers, and so some of the sessions became dull and attendance fell. New ideas and speakers have been constantly in demand for the committee meetings.

Although the original committees and those still in existence are advisory, they have been able to exert some influence on improving services. For example, one woman explained that it was only through the beat committee that the neighborhood was finally able to get action out of the health department to cut weeds and remove trash. Another committee was able to convince the city to approve a sidewalk paving project quickly. The Pleasant Grove Chamber of Commerce worked with one committee to print 50 signs for yards proclaiming "We Report Crime." From this start the Dallas Crime Commission printed 200,000 crime prevention signs and stickers for citywide use. There are numerous examples of committee success, but mostly of a limited nature.

The committee's main objective has been to encourage residents to become the "eyes and ears" for the police department. Not enough funds or police workforce is available to put many officers on foot patrol. Also while patrol cars have the advantage of providing greater mobility and ability to cover larger geographical areas, they do tend to make officers strangers to residents. On the other hand, beat committees bring regular patrol officers into meetings with residents and allow them to become more familiar with one another. Almost daily some residents will contact and assist police. File cards listing home and work phone numbers of members are maintained. Information as to when families in the neighborhood are on vacation or away from home for long periods of time is given to the police and to civilian crime watchers.

In order to improve communications with residents, OGI, paid for the installation of a phone answering service in one chairperson's house at a cost of $200. Since Community Services closes its shop at the end of the day shift, it is important to have someone reply to citizen requests in the evenings when more neighborhood residents are home and want answers.

Committees have also engaged in projects to assist members and families of police officers. Block parties and coffee klatches are still used to bring people together and to raise funds. One successful campaign for the family of a police officer who died of leukemia brought in over $30,000.

*Effectiveness*

**Accomplishments.** Both success and failure have been part of Operation Get Involved. The police department listed accomplishments in a 1973 report prepared by Sergeant John J. Galli of the Community Services Division:

1. Valuable feedback to the department from all districts regarding lack of understanding of our policies and procedures has taken place. This has enabled us to take corrective action before major problems resulted.

2. Information regarding criminal activities and citizen needs have been received by patrol officers participating in committee meetings as well as through the Rumor Control and Information Center.

3. Beats have been divided into small zones by beat committee chairmen and members with a "block captain" responsible for each.

4. Beat committee chairmen and members have conducted public speaking engagements before Parent-Teacher's Associations and civic groups to encourage citizen participation in Operation Get Involved.

5. Yard sign projects in which citizens display signs with crime-stop messages in their front yards have been established on selected beats.

6. Recruits from the police academy have been attending many committee meetings and have been well received by committee members.

7. Several of the committees have conducted letter-writing campaigns supporting the legal changes proposed by the department. We have provided them with pamphlets and a list of state senators and representatives. From this a legislative committee was established to represent all of Operation Get Involved.

8. Better interaction between citizens and police has resulted.

**Proposals.** Community Services also created goals for the 1973–1974 period, many of which were in the process of being implemented when the program was cut back. It proposed to expand the number of beat meetings. It set a goal to increase enrollment in the Identification System by 50 percent over the previous year's 26,000 homes and businesses. It proposed increased education concerning resident and business security, inspection of businesses, rooftop identification, traffic lectures, shoplifting, and crime-reporting seminars, as well as greater efforts to establish more block watch and Helping Hand volunteers.

Completing the transition of Operation Get Involved to a chartered non-profit organization was a principal objective. Moreover, the program was to involve such support as newsletters, more effective promotion flyers, identification cards for beat workers and chairpersons, operating manuals, and training and motivation sessions for patrol officers. But it appears that only a few of these goals and lessons will ever be carried out.

**Phasing Out.** A 2-year LEAA grant of $780,000 provided in 1974 and scheduled to end in 1976 was given for purposes of pursuing some of the crime prevention objectives just listed. However, most of the funds are budgeted for promotional advertising on television and other media. The city has made the decision not to fund or continue direct support of Operation Get Involved. Nowhere is its name even mentioned in the new grant which is designed to decentralize community service officers and regular officers in the five districts for crime prevention purposes. Assistance will be given to community groups already successfully functioning and to some existing beat committees. When an area has been saturated with information, teams working each district will move to another area or interested organization. A central staff will supervise the extensive use of the news media as the prime method to attract interest and encourage attendance at neighborhood meetings. Deputy Chief Souter, in charge of the Patrol Division, believes that this may be the most effective method for getting people out. He has not been impressed with beat committee attendance or the observation that the same people seem to attend most meetings.

**Poor Meeting Attendance.** Operation Get Involved was never fully sold to the majority of police officers. Moreover, one damaging internal study showed such small attendance at beat committee meetings that it was difficult for police officials to conclude that the program should continue. On the other hand, one police official states that the people who eventually brought the program's downfall never participated in it. "They simply saw a head count on attendance figures which showed $10 cost for each participant," he says. "They were confronted with all negative reports and none of the positive ones."

Officers involved closely with the program argue that meeting attendance is no way to judge success or failure. They believe even a few people can make a contribution and carry the workload for a whole area. And when issues arise, attendance increases almost proportionately. Officers believe that the concept alone has encouraged the growth of crime watchers and other volunteers. And there are those who believe that even the chief of police has been isolated and not fully informed about the value of the program. Certain volunteers believe that some officers prefer to keep credit for crime reduction within the police department rather than give any of it to civilian leaders.

**Other Factors**. It may be that other factors have been even more damaging. A few committees (out of a total of 58) which engaged in politics and criticized the City Council on public issues aroused much antagonism. And a few "super-patriots" — seemingly on the verge of vigilantism — especially frightened minority members of City Council. The extreme right-wingers "nosed" around police precincts, dominated beat meetings, and scared off the average citizen. In spite of this behavior, many city officials and police officers still feel that the actions of a few should not be justification to stop an entire program. They believe that it would be better to eliminate the offending committees.

In support of this view, a number of private groups, including the Chamber of Commerce and several other civic bodies, continue to meet and promote the program in certain areas. One division has six out of eighteen committees still functioning, and in other areas approximately fifteen are in operation. A widely respected civilian division chairman, Dan Smith, intends to keep the program going without police direction if necessary. "As a private group, we still insist on the same kind of attention from the police," he says. "And I believe the program really has had an effect on reducing crime."

"There is no doubt in certain neighborhoods crime was reduced," says patrol officer Patterson. "Neighbors got out into the streets, talked to each other, and secured properties. Crime may have risen as a whole in the city, but not as fast in these areas."

*Program Rejuvenation*

Both civilians and police officers speculate about how to rejuvenate the program. Although it may not ever attain its original strength because of the abrupt way it was cut off, they believe it can still be effective in some areas. "A gap exists now between the police and citizens because of this," says Smith. "But, life could be put back into it. However, it would take three to four months to reorganize."

Director of Community Services Edington believes the potential for programs like Operation Get Involved is high. He believes that committee members have been able to criticize and point out problems in exacting terms, whereas this has been difficult sometimes for a government-funded body to do. Letter-writing campaigns and other committee techniques have also proved successful. He says that with proper leadership and resources, one could expect the realistic number of participants in this program to be "100 beats, 100 leaders, and 100 members per beat – 10,000 pairs of eyes and ears to help the police and improve our neighborhoods."

Some officers believe that too much emphasis has been placed on hardware. Once basic hardware has been installed, continued expansion is not cost-effective any longer, they point out. "Helicopters provide one of the finest services, as long as we don't go overboard," says one officer. "We need to spend money for community involvement too."

In this regard, Deputy Chief Souter says, "I feel that Operation Get Involved has done a 'helluva' lot of good." But he is unwilling to say how much support the program should get or what its future is.

Just how much emphasis the city will place on organized community involvement remains to be seen. It may be up to citizens themselves to convince the police department of the potential and value of resident participation.

## Crime Prevention in Simi Valley, California

### Neighborhood Councils

Neighborhood Councils in Simi Valley were formed for a variety of reasons, including neighborhood improvement and crime prevention. Adopted in February 1972, they are typical crime prevention groups, which encourage residents to take basic crime-fighting steps.

The five councils cover the entire city, functioning much like New England town meetings, with executive boards appointed by the City Council for 2-year terms. They deal with traffic safety, crime prevention, community goals, and general city services in this rapidly growing community of 70,000 persons, just north of Los Angeles.

The councils fall under the jurisdiction of the Human Resources Department which, along with the Community Safety Agency (CSA, a police department), is a division of Community Services headed by the chief of police. City organization is modern, with only four major city departments, and police and human resources are uniquely joined in one department in recognition that as much as 80 percent of a police officer's time is spent in providing human services. The combination of law enforcement and human service duties and training has proved an efficient and effective way to operate, according to city officials, especially in a community where there are only 65 sworn officers.

## The Crime Problem

Although the city's population is primarily middle-income with only 2 percent in minority groups, problems abound with runaway children, health, burglary, and delinquency. Because most people work outside the community, burglary is the most serious crime problem, dropping somewhat in summer when more people are around. Strong-arm robberies and forcible rape are infrequent, there being only several occurrences annually. Almost no one fears to walk the streets. The major problem is local residents "ripping off" other residents and youths stealing to play game machines and buy drugs. The California house styles — sliding windows and thin stucco walls — are also conducive to break-ins. And 6-feet fences around pools and backyards shield burglars.

## Effect of Citizen Involvement

Neighborhood council meetings may draw as many as 50 to 70 people, but more often the number is smaller. City Council meets with each of the Neighborhood Council executive committees at least once per year and receives annual reports from each body. Members have learned how to be effective and influential. "Now people attend plan commission meetings," says Mary Spielman, Neighborhood Council coordinator, "and no one can fool them." Even developers have learned to seek approval from Neighborhood Councils before trying to get approval from the Plan Commission. Indeed, they are effective in the reduction of crime through such programs as neighborhood watch, property identification, target hardening, and other techniques.

Councils do not have budgets of their own, but human resource produces a monthly newsletter and bulletins and provides research and two full-time coordinators.

Organization is informal and flexible, which is part of the reason for success, according to former Chief of Police Kenneth Huck, who strongly believes in the involvement of residents in crime prevention programs.

Officer Furnier, head of the burglary division, says, "No program in the U.S. is worth a damn unless the community is involved." The greatest leverage in crime prevention will come from citizen councils, he believes. But you cannot merely flood the community with anticrime leaflets (as happened in Venice, California, for example) and expect that action alone to gain citizen cooperation, Furnier stresses. Continual education, lectures, and meetings are necessary.

Simi Valley considers its victims too. Letters are sent to them and to their neighbors directly after a crime has been committed. Also the victim is visited by Neighborhood Council members to demonstrate their friendship and seek the victim's participation in the local crime prevention programs.

### Administrative Counseling

Perhaps the most unique phase of Simi's crime prevention efforts is administrative counseling. Social contracts are written jointly by police and human resource personnel to resolve disputes between neighbors and establish future guidelines of conduct for them. About 70 agreements are drawn each year and involve such things as delinquency, noisy neighbors, barking dogs, excessive drinking, illegal parking, and marital problems.

Agreements have been written so that neighbors consent to keep in animals after certain hours, or have their children officially counseled, or sit down periodically as friends to resolve differences. When some older youths were disrupting a neighborhood, for example, instead of increased security patrols as requested by residents, an understanding was reached as to whose children were involved, social contracts were agreed upon, and peace was restored to the neighborhood.

Neighborhood Councils have encouraged the use of written agreements and have used their resources to bring the message home to local residents. Successful demonstrations in one neighborhood are passed on to other Neighborhood Councils, and more and more residents are encouraged to join community crime prevention efforts.

# 7

### Citizen Anticrime Crusades and Private Funding Assistance

## Introduction

Citizens can fight crime in many ways. This may come about at the street level through block associations and mobile patrols or at a more centrally organized, committee level through citizen advisory councils and citywide anticrime crusades. Both levels of involvement are desirable, and both are needed to achieve a maximum reduction in crime and the improvement of the criminal justice system.

Because they are motivated from varying sources or interested for different reasons, volunteers and police usually start programs which they feel are best suited for their communities. Many times one program is favored over another because that is what the community is familiar with. Officials and citizens should have knowledge of as many programs as possible. In this regard, citywide crusade committees can review and compare projects for all sections of the city.

### Use of the Crusade

The anticrime crusade can be used to generate citywide interest, direct law enforcement resources into the most important priorities, and stimulate or lobby the city's power structure, legislature, or police officials into action. At the same time, crusades can be used to convince residents of the importance and effect of organizing at the neighborhood level. Mass meetings conducted by citizens in various sections of the community are sometimes more convincing than police-directed campaigns. Police and citizens working together in this effort with singular purpose and determination — professionalism combined with citizen dedication and concern — is even more effective.

### Crusades and Block Associations

One of the problems with centralized anticrime crusades is that they often neglect the highly important aspect of crime prevention in the streets. Citizens at the central level tend to emphasize court reform, police productivity, longer sentences, quick trials for offenders, and many other important issues which usually leave little time to promote active involvement of residents on the blocks where they live. For some it is easier to get involved and stay interested in the glamour of major crime issues than to work largely unnoticed, fighting crime in an apartment building or on a street block. Yet this latter involvement is most important and certainly ought to be included as a major work item on the agenda of any anticrime crusade.

In the cases of the two crusades described in this chapter, so much attention has been directed to the basic reforms of the total criminal justice system that block organization and street crime have taken a secondary role. Sometimes the basic issues of reform must be tackled first, trust developed between police and citizens, and the most modern police techniques introduced before the less spectacular street work activity by citizens can be promoted. Each community should assess at what stage it finds itself, resolve some of the basic issues, and proceed with more direct crime prevention methods. Citywide crusades and block security can originate simultaneously and mature at the same time also.

In two of the most effective citywide anticrime crusade cities — Indianapolis and St. Louis — block group crime prevention activities have not been stressed. Well-organized or concerted efforts to encourage the development and active involvement of street organizations have been lacking. After many years of citizen anticrime work, active resident involvement in street and home security is only now being stressed and its importance recognized.

In the past, most cities concentrated on better street lighting, property security, more police officers, look-out towers, and passive kinds of neighborhood watch, but neglected what many believe may be the single most important element — active resident involvement at the neighborhood level. Some leaders still discourage the active involvement of citizens because of the inherent danger to the individual; yet in the functioning of most block clubs, dangers are minimized and the value of their work is worth the effort. Indeed crime crusades can be a valuable method for publicizing and generating public interest in block associations.

*Initiation and Membership.*

Anticrime crusades can be organized by local government or private organizations. In the past, women's groups, neighborhood improvement associations, newspapers, and city officials have been prime movers in their development. Some crusades claim membership of over 100 organizations and 25,000 to 50,000 citizens. But leadership usually stems from a small core of a dozen or so persons and perhaps 100 or fewer active members who regularly participate in crusade assignments. Sometimes this small number is sufficient to affect the community substantially.

Crusade participants are usually women, of all age groups and income levels and races; however, most tend to be white, middle-aged, and in the middle and upper-middle income brackets. When organizing a crusade, greater efforts need to be placed on recruiting minorities, the poor, and males. Crime is prevalent in poverty areas, but the poor have to be shown how membership in an anti-crime crusade might benefit them. For some it is too nebulous. Block organization and observance, however, is one method of increasing the range of citizen involvement.

## Publicity

Publicity is the crusade's most powerful tool. Members research, observe, and expose corruption and ineptitude. It would be difficult to accomplish this without the interest and help of the news media. Although needed as well, pamphlets and conferences — regular devices of the crusade — are less influential on the public. Officials fear the press which many times forces them into action.

## Organization

Organization is not complex. A chairperson and board of directors are elected by the membership at an annual meeting. In some instances the terms of office are not even definite, and the number of board members will vary with the interest different groups show in specific crime projects. It is very much informal, the primary purpose being to keep members interested and active in any suitable crime prevention project by means of personal leadership and group motivation.

## Budget

Budgets may come from two sources — government or private contributions. Usually annual dues of about $10, civic and business donations, and fund-raising bazaars and sales are the means to cover costs of mailing and other minor expenses. However, most recently some local governments have taken an interest in the work of crusades and would like to see them expand their services and organize resident groups in each neighborhood to fight crime. A well-organized, citywide campaign of this sort requires some staff. The necessary resources are usually only available from government funds.

## Goals

Goals revolve around reducing crime; improving the criminal justice system, including the courts, probation, and corrections; assisting police; and encouraging citizens to help themselves. Objectives naturally vary from one community to the next because conditions are different and priorities constantly shifting. For example, one crusade's set of goals for one year were as follows:

1. Better police protection, more beat police officers, and improved police-community relations
2. Improved juvenile detention and rehabilitation centers . . . and, at the same time, a citywide program of help for juveniles to keep them in school and out of trouble
3. Demolition of more vacant and unsafe buildings
4. Better lighting in streets, alleys, parks, and private areas
5. Improvement of moral values and social conduct

### Indianapolis Women's Anticrime Crusade

The first and perhaps the most effective anticrime crusade is functioning in Indianapolis. Back in 1962, when an elderly retired school teacher died after being knocked down outside her apartment house by a 15-year-old purse-grabber, the people of Indianapolis became quite alarmed and prepared to do something about crime. Street crimes, muggings, robberies, and purse-grabbings became daily occurrences on the streets of Indianapolis, happening even in broad daylight in what had previously been generally regarded as "safe" parts of the city. But the news of the killing of a woman in a purse snatching sparked the first organized citizen effort to do something about street crimes.

At the suggestion of one of its women's-page writers, the *Indianapolis News* agreed to host a luncheon for about 30 women, most of them presidents of women's organizations in the city. At that luncheon, the women committed themselves and, to the extent they could, their organizations to a campaign against crime. And the Indianapolis Anticrime Crusade was born, under the sponsorship of the *Indianapolis News*.

One of the first visible results of that organizational meeting was a printed flyer that urged Indianapolis women to "Ask your friends to join the Anticrime Crusade to make the streets safe for women." The flyer listed what it described as some simple rules recommended by the Indianapolis Police Department: Don't invite crime in your car. Don't open your home to crime. To prevent attack, don't do various things. If attacked, scream. Never display money. The flyer concluded by urging persons to "send ideas for fighting crime in Indianapolis, to the Anticrime Crusade at the *Indianapolis News.*"

During those formative months, the organization was publicly identified and generally referred to as The News' Anticrime Crusade. But several years ago, the *News* disassociated itself from the Anticrime Crusade, at least formally, though the newspaper still gives the Anticrime Crusade good coverage in its news columns and occasionally provides administrative help.

Late in 1974, James E. Pauloski, public relations director for the *Indianapolis News* and the *Indianapolis Star,* said, "It was necessary for the *News* to sponsor the Anticrime Crusade when it was getting started, but its leaders were told their group would eventually have to achieve independence. This it did about five years ago."

*Membership*

In its publicity, the Anticrime Crusade often refers to "50,000 volunteer women" united against crime, or some variation on this theme. It is possible that about 50,000 women have been involved in the work of the Anticrime Crusade, but not all as members and not on every project. Rather, they participate when called upon and when the project interests them. The rest of the time most are just members of various other Indianapolis clubs, churches, and organizations that affiliate with the Anticrime Crusade on different projects.

Membership in the various organizations varies widely. The Indianapolis Council of Women includes 129 groups and about 25,000 women. The Seventh District Federation of Clubs involves another 2,000 or 3,000 women. The Citizens Forum, Inc. claims several hundred block clubs with an almost undeterminable number of members. Then, there are smaller groups, such as the Indianapolis Branch of the American Association of University Women, the Altrusa Club, the Business and Professional Women's Club, the Welfare Club, the Needlework Guild, and the Veterans of Foreign Wars Auxiliary, to mention but a few.

These and other groups have worked with the Anticrime Crusade. But the principal leadership has come from a fairly small group of women — and perhaps most of all from one person, Margaret More Post, who helped found the Anticrime Crusdae in 1962 and has been its coordinator for all 12 years of its existence. People familiar with the crusade say she is a big reason, if not *the* reason, that the Anticrime Crusade is alive and active today. Women (and some men) of all ages and races and most income levels are in the crusade. But most of the participants and leaders are white, middle-aged, and in the middle and upper-middle income brackets.

A notable exception is Mattie Coney, founder and head of the Citizens Forum, Inc., a biracial group dedicated to promoting good citizenship and building pride and self-respect in poor, inner-city neighborhoods. Mattie Coney is black and taught school in predominantly black schools in Indianapolis for more than 30 years. The Citizens Forum, Inc. helped form more than 2,000 block clubs in all areas of Indianapolis. It got the city to initiate a heavy-trash pick-up system in Indianapolis, and it has conducted numerous rat-control programs, clean-up, fix-up, paint-up campaigns, and city beautification projects.

*Organization and Budget*

The Crusade has a chairperson and board of directors composed of a dozen women, most of whom head or have headed specific projects under the Anti-crime Crusade umbrella. There are no definite terms of office, and the number of board members varies with the interest of groups in specific projects.

Only about 100 persons pay the annual dues of $10. Board meetings are held infrequently and sometimes only on the telephone. The Anticrime Crusade has no paid staff and no office. The mailing address (5343 North Arlington Avenue, Indianapolis, Indiana 46226) is the home address of Mattie Post.

Myra Wirenius, who has been chairwoman for more than two years, said she is likely to remain as chairwoman as long as she remains interested and feels she can make a contribution. The first chairwoman, C.B. LaDine, served for al-most 10 years.

Funding raising is informal and money is raised as needed, in whatever ways the membership feels are most appropriate. Much of the money is contributed by the individuals involved. Other funds come from businesses and associations that have an interest in a project of the Anticrime Crusade, from honoraria received by members of the group's speakers' bureau, and from chili suppers, bazaars, book review programs, and other fund-raising events conducted by affiliated organizations. The latest newsletter of the Anticrime Crusade, for example, was printed by Indiana National Bank. It was addressed and mailed by the *Indianapolis News;* the Anticrime Crusade paid the postage.

*Philosophy*

The Women's Anticrime Crusade has never marched on city hall in protest. Instead, its leaders go to City Hall with advance appointments to sit down with city officials and talk about how they can help the police department or other parts of the city administration. They also seek help from private groups, such as the Indianapolis Chamber of Commerce, the Retail Merchants Association, and the Insurance Institute of Indiana.

Mattie Post said, "The Anticrime Crusade asks the advice of police *before* undertaking projects. And we work *with,* not against, city and state officials. Community cooperation has been the thesis of our work. And if we've had any success at all, that's been the basis of it."

The Anticrime Crusade literature describes the movement as "biracial, interfaith, nonpolitical in character. We work locally, statewide and nationally with the administration in office."

Mattie Post is strongly opposed to the use of federal funds to operate groups such as the Anticrime Crusade or to deal with the kinds of local prob-lems. in which the Anticrime Crusade gets involved. So the Anticrime Crusade does not seek, nor would it accept, federal grants. However, some of its affiliated organizations do use government funds.

*Programs and Results*

The Anticrime Crusade has initiated a variety of different projects over the last 12 years, all in some way aimed at helping control crime in Indianapolis. Projects have included such things as adding thousands of new lights to the city's streets. working with dropouts, distributing over 200,000 leaflets on self-protection, stimulating Spruce-up-the-City projects, and sponsoring property identification efforts and national town meetings on crime prevention.

Following is a discussion of the major projects and some of the results achieved.

**Court Watching**. This was one of the Anticrime Crusade's first major projects. The program continues, although not with the emphasis given in earlier years. Couples work together — in each of Indianapolis' municipal, criminal, and juvenile courts — to maintain daily records for their own review and evaluation. Volunteers use mimeographed sheets to record their observations. They record whether the judge is present or whether there was a *pro tempore* filling in. They score delays and continuances and the parties most often responsible for them, and, of course, the types of cases and how they are handled.

Almost immediately judges recognized that there was a greater dignity in the courtroom because the women were observing; the judges credited the court watchers with this improvement.

Comparative notes about parallel courts, according to members, aided greatly in helping to get a packet of bills on court reform passed in the 1969 Indiana General Assembly.

The Anticrime Crusade reports that its members sat in on more than 200,000 cases and played a major part in a number of court reforms. Also they report that the prosecuting attorney's deputies now prepare their cases more thoroughly. Among the recent reforms resulting wholly or in part from the work of the court watchers are the following:

1. Establishment of a presiding judge or municipal court, providing more uniformity and responsibility for the city's municipal courts.
2. More specialization in the courts, with certain judges to hear alcoholics and premental cases with follow-up counseling.
3. Drastic cut in "judgment withheld" cases.
4. Hallway bailiff named to clear loiterers from the court halls.
5. Judges appear on time and wear robes.
6. Arresting officers are absent less often.

7. Fewer *pro tempore* judges and fewer delays.

8. Permanent driver improvement school established.

**Work with Police.** Below is the Anticrime Crusade's own statement regarding its work with police. Although written about three years ago, it is still accurate and a good indication of their attitude and relationship with the police.

1. We have supported increases in police salaries. . . .

2. We have supported legislation which has provided for a large area of recruiting, allowed more funds for uniforms and provided for a police academy.

3. We provide a quarterly award in cooperation with Exchange Clubs for police work beyond the ordinary.

4. We assist with a Police and Fireman Appreciation Dinner annually.

5. We had the first tea in the nation honoring policemen's wives. Try this. It's so easy to do and means so much!

6. Women's organizations throughout our city take turns serving as hostesses at receptions for graduating police recruits. Sometimes as many as 400 members of their families and friends attend these events. Until we had receptions, the graduates had to congratulate themselves.

7. We attend classes, panel discussions, seminars, Safety Board meetings, City-County Council meetings and hearings, every function that would provide a forum of learning about police activity and a better understanding of the department. The police chief invited our chairman and coordinator to spend 48 hours in the police department – and they did and talked at all 30 roll calls.

8. Consistently we have maintained a hands-off policy on daily operations of the department, insisting instead that those charged with this responsibility do their jobs well.

9. Crusade women initiated a scholarship program for policemen and arranged for Indiana University credit courses to be taught in the police wing classrooms of Indianapolis' new City-County Building. A new department of police administration has been developed at Indiana University-Purdue University at Indianapolis.

**Assistance to Other Cities.** In 1971, the Anticrime Crusade published a booklet designed to tell people in other cities what the women of Indianapolis had accomplished and how other could do something similar. The booklet was entitled *The Indianapolis Anti-Crime Crusade of 50,000 Volunteer Women Offers a Blueprint for the Nation in Crime Prevention* and covered the following major areas:

It is unwise to jump on a horse and ride in all directions. (A wise plan is to name committees of two or three women to meet with the various public officials who aleady are working on crime prevention – the mayor, the police chief, the sheriff, judges, prosecuting attorney, probation head, corrections head, school administrator, church heads, community service council director, etc.) Ask to meet at the convenience of the public official. Suggest that the committee would like to know some of the things which are being done to curb crime. Then ask "How can we help you?"

The list of things you can do will be so long that you will need 3,000 women instead of 30. Each woman who attends the first meeting will want to enlist the help of one or more organizations to which she belongs. The women will be glad to help when they know that there are jobs to suit every talent, every age. They can spend one hour a week or 10 hours a day. But, as (former) Attorney General Mitchell points out, we can accomplish just so much with legislation and big grants of federal funds. Unless citizens on every street in America look at the problems in their own community and begin to solve them, we cannot curb crime.

Have patience and be diplomatic. Some parts of the problem are fast-moving. You can get a light in your alley overnight. You can get a dropout back in school in a few days. You can go with a policeman to make a speech to 500 women on self-protection. But court reform, this may take six years, as it did in Indianapolis.

You will want to tailor your program to the needs of your city, but the Indianapolis plan will be a guideline in most communities. You can begin one program, two or even three. It is unwise to bein all 14 projects at once. You will need very little money to begin the program. All of the funds needed for the vast stay-in-school program in Indianapolis were made by clubs, sororities, auxiliaries, church circles and various groups which sponsored a bazaar, a chili supper, a benefit book review for "John" or "Mary." Individuals and organizations also contributed. Tabs for mimeographing, printing and mailing can be picked up by individuals, industries, foundations or organizations interested in making your city a better place in which to live. Mimeographing may be done on school projects by the schools.

The Indianapolis program is made up of 14 divisions, each headed by a capable volunteer. A general chairman, and a coordinator, with the division heads make up the board of directors. The division heads are fairly autonomous, taking the responsibility of their work, calling on their volunteers whenever there is need for immediate or long-range work. The board meets approximately once a month in business sessions and sometimes has telephone meetings. Crime prevention is often of immediate concern. Action may be needed now! Approximately every three months, some 60 persons convene — leaders of Crusade, public officials particularly concerned with projects at hand, and other volunteers who have special reports. Almost every women's organization in Indianapolis is working the Crusade in some manner.

The Anticrime Crusade is a movement, not an organization. It is biracial, interfaith, nonpolitical in character. We work locally, statewide and nationally with the administration in office.

We work on principles, not issues.

**Women United Against Rape.** In August 1973, the Anticrime Crusade and the Mayor's Task Force on Women organized a communitywide meeting to bring interested groups and individuals together into a new body called Women United Against Rape. The meeting was pretty much a response to reports that forcible rape had become the fastest-growing crime of violence in the nation.

In little more than a year, the Women United Against Rape succeeded in getting a new state law passed, two women deputy prosecutors assigned full time to prosecuting rape cases, policewomen used to interview rape victims, more sensitivity and better cooperation by hospitals in handling rape victims and evidence in rape cases, and a great deal more public awareness of the need for self-protection and the problems of ensuring justice in rape cases.

The rape law, passed by the 1974 state legislature, was introduced by two state senators from Indianapolis at the request of Women United Against Rape. It prohibits suspended sentences being given to convicted rapists. It mandates determinate sentences for convicted rapists, instead of indeterminate 2-to-21-year terms, as previously set out by Indiana law. And it mandates sentencing of sex deviates convicted of rape to correctional institutions instead of assignment to mental hospitals. No change was made in the procedure of assigning to mental hospitals alleged rapists judged by psychiatrists as "mentally incapable of standing trial." Also the same procedure remains for those judged "sexual psychopaths."

The reasoning behind assigning convicted rapists to correctional institutions rather than mental hospitals was emphasized by one of the prosecutors. "We have had a consistent problem of almost immediate walk-away from mental hospitals of sex deviates convicted of rape," Leroy New, Marion County (Indianapolis) chief deputy prosecutor, said in support of the bill's passage. If sex deviates convicted of rape need and wish psychiatric and/or psychological treatment, he said, help can be arranged in correctional institutions.

At the request of the Women United Against Rape, the Marion County prosecutor assigned two women deputy prosecutors full time to the prosecution of rape cases. And the police assigned policewomen to the task of questioning rape victims. Police Lieutenant Ron Bates said, "the use of the two policewomen has resulted in more openness [on the part of the rape victims] because they are talking to women." Also, the women have gotten the Indianapolis hospitals to do a better job of providing information and evidence to police following examination and treatment of rape victims in hospital emergency rooms. And, Bates believes, "that helps with the case in court."

Police and hospitals have coordinated a uniform checklist of tests for determining the health of the victim and for apprehension of the alleged suspect. Hospitals have been supplied by the police with a lock box to be kept in the vicinity of the initial examining area. After completion of the patient's examination, the slides, swabs, and washings are marked with the patient's identification. These and clothing that might be used as evidence are placed in the box which is then sent to the police crime laboratory where tests are processed at no cost to the victim. The contents of the box remain at the Indianapolis Police Department for presentation in any subsequent criminal court proceeding.

The Anticrime Crusade claims to be the "first city in the nation to develop the hospital-police-prosecutor plan for the victim, so that she has no fear of reporting a rape immediately."

Presently the Anticrime Crusade is preparing to ask the Indiana General Assembly to pass another bill — this one to prevent the victim's past private life, or previous sexual conduct, from being brought up in a rape trial. The law they propose would permit the defense to bring out only relevant information bearing on the trial.

In addition, a proposal for a specialized training center for rape prevention has been made by Women United Against Rape, in cooperation with the Center for Criminal Justice Training at Indiana University and the Criminal Justice Planning Agency of Indiana.

The proposal, which is now before the Law Enforcement Assistance Administration in Washington, calls for ten 3-day specialized training sessions for 500 police officers (50 at each session). These sessions would deal with the handling of rape cases and the need to improve coordination between police and citizen programs and rape and rape prevention.

About 1,100 individuals and organizations are on the mailing list of the Women United Against Rape. This project has drawn at least moral support from virtually every women's organization in the Indianapolis area. It is by far the most broadly based project in which the Anticrime Crusade has been involved.

In addition to the efforts to change and improve the system of handling rape investigations and prosecution, the Women United Against Rape have given wide distribution to information on self-protection for women. This has been done through brochures, the mass media, and speakers provided to other groups and organizations.

**Other Projects from the Women United Against Rape.** In another area, concentration on individual protection, the Anticrime Crusade has begun a new effort to improve safety (primarily for women) in parking lots and garages, public buildings, shopping centers, industries, and other places where a person might be particularly vulnerable to attack.

On October 17, 1974, security officers from businesses, industries, shopping centers, hospitals, colleges, universities, and elsewhere were invited to meet with representatives of the Indianapolis Police Department and the Women United Against Rape. The meeting was held in the City-County Building auditorium, and several hundred persons were present. A list of security suggestions, most of them gathered from other cities, was presented; some of these are now in the process of being implemented.

1. More lights on streets and in alleys.
2. Closed-circuit TV for use in shopping centers, parking garages, elevators, and possibly in stores.
3. Escort service to cars for security of personnel working at night, for hospital visitors, etc.
4. All personnel helping with parking or other facilities wear large badges identifying them, so that visitors know who is directing them.
5. Security towers in parking lots. (Eastern Airlines in Miami has one. And

the Anticrime Crusade has had one designed.)

6. Greater use of police and fire call boxes.
7. Call boxes in shopping centers.
8. Small alarm systems that will ring in adjoining businesses.
9. A new business in Houston features a system for a home or small business in which the panic button is carried in hand or pocket. If a woman walking a dog, for example, becomes frightened or if there is a medical emergency, she can press the button and an alarm system in her home is activated; then, in turn, someone at home reports to police.
10. A school system in the East which has been plagued with vandalism and actual attacks on teachers provides each teacher with an escort service to her car — and a pencil with a "top-press" can send an alert to a central location. Teachers can also "talk" into the pencil.
11. On a university campus, small telephones are mounted on posts, and students fearing attacks can knock off phones, thus alerting a centrally located place to their danger.

Early in 1974, an Indianapolis architectural firm, working with Women United Against Rape and the Indianapolis police, designed a security tower from which round-the-clock guards could survey an entire parking lot. The women say the tower is suitable for use in parking lots near shopping centers, hospitals, university campuses, industrial plants, retail stores, fairgrounds, airports, auditoriums, and wherever else large areas are used by cars and people. Credit for the tower idea is given to Deputy Chief Ralph Lumpkin, who is in charge of the homicide and robbery divisions of the Indianapolis Police Department.

*Relations with Police*

The Anticrime Crusade's relationship with the Indianapolis Police Department is excellent. Police Major Winston Churchill, who was chief of the Indianapolis Police Department from 1968 until 1974, put it this way: "The police are extremely happy for anyone who will say 'we love you' and mean it. And they [the women of the Anticrime Crusade] have put time and effort where it counts." Churchill said that the Anticrime Crusade has been "extremely valuable" to the Police Department. "They brought about some uniform changes that we wanted to get made for years," he said. "They got it done."

As an example, he said, the police used to have to wear a three-quarter-length winter coat, like a pee-jacket. This made it impossible for an officer, particularly one in a patrol car, to draw his/her service revolver. The situation was so bad that many officers carried a second gun in a coat pocket where they could reach it quickly in an emergency. "They [the Anticrime Crusade women] convinced the city it was 'stupid.' That's just the word they used. And the rule was changed." Now the Indianapolis police wear a short jacket that permits easy access to their sidearms.

"In the early days," Churchill said, "a lot of police scoffed at them. But we soon learned they were serious. I used to let them use the police conference room, and it was not uncommon to see 25 ladies in there addressing letters or something."

Churchill praised the teas the women held for officers' wives and the receptions for the recruit class graduations: "Those are the nice little things." But he went on the say that he appreciates the Anticrime Crusade most because "it's got a hell of a lot of clout." He said, "They support law enforcement in the state legislature. And I never saw legislation go through the legislature as fast as that antirape bill did. It even had an emergency clause [so it went into effect immediately upon being signed by the governor] ."

Much the same opinion was echoed by Indianapolis Police Deputy Chief Raymond Stratton. He said the Anticrime Crusade does "a pretty decent job." He said, "They got the Crime Alert number started. [This is a phone number to be used by the public to report a crime quickly.] They got the rape program. They got a lot of women doing more to protect themselves. They don't come into contact with the men on the street very much, but it would be good if they did. When they were sitting in the courts taking notes, it did some good. It kept those judges on the ball."

The Anticrime Crusade is best known and most respected by the top brass with whom they work most closely, but support for the Crusade is widespread on the Indianapolis police force. This is probably not too surprising for a group whose philosophy is "it is far easier to scold the chief of police for failing to catch criminals than to take the responsibility for setting the moral climate of the community high enough to discourage criminal activity of any kind."

*Conclusions*

Although operating informally and with only about 100 active members, the Anticrime Crusade has been highly effective in enlisting and motivating other groups and individuals quickly and easily in community crime prevention projects. Even though much of the group's success can be attributed to the generation of publicity, it has conducted many worthwhile projects, which both the public and police believe have helped to reduce crime. The middle- and higher-income areas have been the main participants and have probably benefitted the most; however, there has been some impact on the black community. Critics say its answers to street crime are too simplistic and maintenance of interest in the Crusade based too much on a theory of fear. But overall, the Women's Anticrime Crusade has been successful and is making an impact on reducing crime and improving justice. Its purposes and methods are worthwhile pursuits for volunteer organizations in many other cities and counties across the nation.

## St. Louis Women's Crusade against Crime

Another experience has been taking place in St. Louis, stimulated by and largely following the Indianapolis program. There are also some other similar programs operating in cities across the nation. The St. Louis project provides the opportunity to discuss the basic elements of anticrime crusades.

### Purpose and Goals

In demonstration of his trust for the St. Louis Women's Crusade against Crime (WCAC), a young offender recently approached one of its members, Martha Webb, for help rather than going to the police. "He trusted me because I was a member, and he knew the organization helped people," stated Martha Webb. "He told me that he felt that I could be of some help to him. He said himself that that is why he came to me."

Martha Webb epitomizes what the WCAC attempts to do and what it is — a deterrent to crime by utilizing positive community efforts and at the same time a basis for developing trust between the community and the police. In short, WCAC acts as a catalyst to bring together the community and the forces of law and order.

The fact that a man who had just shot and killed another man went not to the police, but to a woman he had met briefly only once because of her affiliation with an organization, reflects the prestige and the trust WCAC managed to generate in only its second year of existence. It also symbolizes the hunger some segments of the population have for an intermediary with the police.

"We try to get the citizens to know the police," explained Mrs. McClellan, cochairperson. "We want the police also to know what the citizens are thinking about, what they expect, what they demand."

The WCAC was the result of a group of West End St. Louis women who organized in September, 1969 as the Women for City Living (WCL). WCL, while concerning itself with spiraling crime rates in the west central area of the city, devoted much of its efforts to area beautification. Still in existence, WCL now almost exclusively devotes its attention to the latter.

On January 15, 1970, at the request of then Mayor Alfonso J. Cervantes, a group of about 100 women from throughout the city assembled in his office to help promote an anticrime bond issues package and a tax increase to help finance it. "The mayor asked us to do this and help in getting a bond issue and tax increase passed to pay for additional police officers, street lighting, and new juvenile detention facilities," Mrs. McClellan recalled.

Mrs. McClellan and Mrs. Prince J. Claiborne were named cochairpersons. They selected the name, Women's Crusade Against Crime, modeled after a similar organization in Indianapolis which had achieved, they said, remarkable success in similar endeavors. It was to be a volunteer organization, with no membership dues. Donations, however, were sought to cover costs of educational leaflets and brochures.

The list of honorary chairpersons and members of the board of directors was impressive. Wives of former mayors and other civic and business leaders lent their names.

The WCAC's first appeal for public support came less than a month later. "We want to put *woman power* together for immediate action, through individuals and through every possible women's organization. We must have the help of every woman in St. Louis to fight the crime and blight that is hurting our neighbors and ruining our city."

The philosophy of maintaining a high profile was to become one of several lines of reasoning behind the WCAC that were to endure. Its members would become lobbyists, a pressure group, thorns in the sides of reluctant city and police officials. Emphasis was placed on law enforcement as it existed, without trying to transplant the system to volunteers. Patrols or active street involvement were discouraged as too dangerous and classified as being primarily police work not suited to inexperienced volunteers.

In the early days, as now, WCAC worked closely with the police department, seeking its advice on how to proceed, where to concetrate, and where it could be most effective.

The department already had established police-community relations organizations in its nine police districts, and WCAC decided to cooperate, urging its members to become active. The department was soliciting block watchers, and WCAC agreed to help. Hundreds of block watchers were recruited, and, of course, they became sympathetic to WCAC in the process.

In addition, in 1974 and 1975, WCAC encouraged the St. Louis County Police Department and many municipalities in the county to adopt the Block Watcher Program because "this would provide all police departments with citizen eyes and ears throughout the metropolitan area."

*Membership and Budget*

Most of the originators of WCAC are still members. Mrs. McClellan reports that from a small core of about 50 to 70 active members, an organization of about 2,000 in "varying degrees of activity" and about "200 to 300 members who are really active" now exists. WCAC has a mailing list of about 8,000. There are 44 members on its board of directors, 50 percent of whom are black. The annual budget is $40,000 (90 percent through an LEAA grant) for four salaried personnel, at a cost of $20,000, and the remainder for its newspaper *Crusade Courier* and other printing and office expenses.

*Projects*

WCAC has concentrated in the areas of police, courts, corrections, and juvenile delinquency. Results were overwhelmingly successful in its Drug Sweep Out Campaign, which identified drug pushers by the use of discreet pipelines of informants. Secret Witness was another successful crime-informing project whereby callers were assigned numbers, and names were not used.

In *Lady, Be Careful,* 40,000 pamphlets were distributed describing seven rules of safety, Whistle Stop and Operation Identification techniques, and how to deal with purse snatching. And in cooperation with the Women's Auxiliary of St. Louis University School of Law, WCAC distributed 200,000 copies of *Youth and the Law,* designed to ameliorate juvenile programs. Its *Kids 'N Kops Day* attracted 10,000 youngsters and 74 surrounding police departments.

A scoreboard is kept in WCAC offices to show progress on legislation and in such areas as improving police training, courts, correctional institutions, and related fields. A good deal of advice and various methods were provided by representatives from the Indianapolis Women's Anticrime Crusade. Now St. Louis is publicizing its techniques and experiences for the benefit of other cities.

*Lobbying for Law*

It is axiomatic in WCAC that they go to the power structure to get results. Members say that "to get anything done, you have to go right to the top." It is a tenet that has existed from the very beginning.

When the St. Louis Crime Commission held its organizational meeting in April 1970, WCAC was there. Mrs. McClellan "sat in on the . . . meeting — only because she pressured the powers politely but firmly as to the logic of WCAC being a part of any crime commission." That pressure, she explained, consisted mostly of a "lot of badgering" and "convincing them that we were sincere and here to stay."

It is with near brazenness that the WCAC approaches its work. "We are trying to help bring people and the system together," Mrs. McClellan explained, "so we go right to the top."

Judges often feel the wrath of WCAC. "We work with the judges," Mrs. McClellan said. "Sometimes, I'll call one up and say, 'Hey, you're not doing this right.' And they'll listen. . . . We are a lobbying group, lobbying against crime. The mayor once said to us that you women are into everything. We try to be. If we stir up a little controversy, then that's what we're here for. Sometimes it takes a bit of controversy for people to wake up. They can't fire us. We're volunteers."

While WCAC does not flaunt itself, it is unafraid to push for what it wants. Mrs. McClellan explained, "At first, the police were skeptical. They worried that we were just a militant group there to shame them. But now they've seen that we are responsible and some of them have become our staunchest supporters. . . They fear and respect us now. They know we got a little power and we'll use it."

Some of the power WCAC possesses comes from its several thousand members, but some of it is also derived from one of its greatest lobbying successes which resulted in membership on a key decision-making board. One of its members, Mrs. Salees W. Seddon, who has been active in the Women for City Living and many other community projects, was appointed to the board of police commissioners in February 1973 by Missouri Governor Christopher S. Bond. She became the first woman member of this civilian board, which operates the department, determines policy, promotes officers, and disciplines members.

This was "our shining hour — the first woman commissioner in the city's history. All this time we had been plotting how and what we wanted the police commissioners to do and how to reach them. Our worries vanished overnight!" Mrs. McClellan smiled. One of Mrs. Seddon's first acts was to enroll in the Police Academy "to see what went on there and whether it needed changes."

Other successes soon followed. Celeste Ruwwe, the only police department member who is associated with WCAC, was promoted to a sergeant shortly after Mrs. Seddon became a board member. More women were recruited as commissioned personnel. Mayor John Poelker was approached by WCAC recently and told: A factor in the deterioration of our neighborhoods . . . is the number of taverns and liquor stores allowed to operate. Juveniles are seen drinking beer on the streets, and we suspect they are buying it in these stores, all over the city. What is the answer to this problem? What needs to be done to solve this problem? We would appreciate any answers so we could assist in remedying this bad situation." The group's aggressiveness continues to be exerted on key officials.

Chief of Police Eugene J. Camp said recently: "The Women's Crusade Against Crime is requesting the formation of Neighborhood Police Units — special teams of police officers who would become familiar with streets, stores, residents and entire crime patterns in selected high crime areas. The neighborhoods of St. Louis . . . cannot survive unless we have such a joint citizen-police effort on a continuing basis. Citizens need and want police officers who will become as familiar with the problems as they, themselves, are. We would appreciate hearing your views on such a plan."

It was more or less tactfully meant to be a subtle suggestion from the chief of police to other authorities that the WCAC wanted, and expected, action.

Neither the state nor Missouri supreme court officials are immune to WCAC's approach to solving problems. Missouri Attorney General John C. Danforth was invited to speak on a courts seminar, sponsored by WCAC, in March 1973. After explaining some of the problems in the court system, Mrs. McClellan commented in what could be construed as a tacit warning: "I tell you these incidents to illustrate what we women are finding and the citizen-pressure we are trying to place on the proper officials, but the problems seem insurmountable and we are running out of energy."

Or, in working on reform of the bail bond system, Mrs. McClellan told Missouri Supreme Court Judge James A. Finch: "We feel your assistance is urgently needed . . . to bring order out of chaos. I would look forward to hearing from you, soon."

Perhaps the WCAC's official position on its future programs best sums up its philosophy:

Communication between police and courts, courts and corrections, police and youth, any combination of the four ingredients is possible. They are all interrelated and they can only function at their peak when they work in harmony with one another. Above all, the system must seek out ways to communicate with the public. Its responsibility is to all citizens. For, we must face it, the criminal justice system is far from perfect. We must all work for progressive improvement.

*Observations*

WCAC has been successful for a number of reasons: (1) it does not attempt to be a substitute for the police, but rather to complement them; (2) it presents itself as an ally of the police, often courting them, frequently championing better working conditions; (3) it rarely is antagonistic toward the police, themselves, limiting its criticisms to deficiencies in police services, training, and administration; (4) while militant in nature, it is cautiously so, but is unafraid to attack "sacred cows" of the system; and (5) it is an advocate of law and order and not disorder.

Its success with the community seems to be the result of several things: performing as an advocate in matters which concern great segments of the public; satisfying a public craving for someone with whom to talk freely; filling a vacuum between those who might need police services (or come in contact with police) and the police themselves; and taking direct action, rather than presenting only a plethora of words. In brief, it has been a successful citizen's ombudsman in law enforcement.

**The New York City Police Foundation, Inc.**

Many times citizens want to know how they can help in reducing crime. Sometimes their action may take the form of a donation. But if money is given, one wishes to know that it was used properly and without influence. Impartial, trustworthy citizens organized to collect and distribute funds is one answer. The New York City Police Foundation is such a unique group. Other cities or private groups may wish to adopt a similar program. Resources can be used for many private ventures as well, including home and street security.

Spurred by lack of understanding and cooperation between citizens and the police department and by revelations of police corruption (brought out by the Knapp Commission's investigation of the New York City Police Department), a small nucleus of private citizens formed the independent, not-for-profit New York City Police Foundation in November 1971. The basic concept of the Foundation is to function as a vehicle for community support of the police department, for improving police effectiveness, and for the funding of police department projects not otherwise possible under the city's restrictive line item budget.

The solicitation of funds is ongoing. It is done with the help of a prestigious board of trustees composed of business persons and civic leaders. Donors remain anonymous and expect no favors in return for their contributions. The purpose of this is to end direct solicitation of funds by the police department for any purpose, however well meaning, and it is one of the chief objectives of the Foundation.

*Purposes*

The foundation's purposes are as follows:

1. To improve communications and relations between the police department and the public it serves, including all the various communities in the city.
2. To initiate studies and programs for the purpose of improving the performance and effectiveness of the police department.
3. To aid the New York City Police Department in its continuing campaign against internal corruption by providing a legitimate, tax-exempt vehicle for the receipt of gifts from those who wish to benefit the police department, directly or indirectly.
4. To provide funds and resources for the police department which would not otherwise be available.

*The Budget and Staff*

Annual contributions have varied since the Foundation was formed. In 1972, $52,680 was raised; in 1973, $119,840; and in 1974 over $133,000. The 1974 donations have already exceeded the 1973 figure. Fund-raising campaigns so far have been low key, and there are no stringent budget targets.

A majority of funds are used to fund projects. About 60 percent of the cash budget is for grants to the police department. These grants rose from

$22,950 in 1972 to $74,350 in 1973. The remaining 40 percent of budget goes for salaries to a full-time administrative director, administrative assistant, and secretary, plus normal office and other expenses. Some office supplies plus all legal and accounting services are provided without charge by the Spear and Hill legal firm where free office space is also donated. The two rooms provided free to the Foundation plus receptionist services and the use of meeting and other facilities are significant noncash contributions. Counting these donations and the numerous hours the board, public relations firms, and other professionals contribute to the Foundation, the actual administrative percentage of budget is higher. Nevertheless, emphasis is placed on donated services and holding down administrative costs.

Importantly, the operation has reached a point where additional cash contributions would be almost entirely disbursed in the form of grants and scholarships, the major reason for the Foundation's existence. Furthermore, Administrative Director Cornelia Perry says that public interest in the Foundation is rising and should have the effect of increasing contributions and therefore decreasing the percentage of administrative costs.

The Foundation's primary function is to dispense funds. It does not operate projects. If it did, personnel requirements would be considerably larger.

*Setting Project Priorities*

Determining grant priorities represents a large share of the Foundation's work. The administrative director meets monthly with the police department's program and policies inspectors and other officers to determine police needs.

After an initial assessment of needs, Perry and Eliot H. Lumbard, chairman of the board, make recommendations to the Foundation's executive committee of five, which meets about six times annually to approve grants. The full board of eighteen meets about four times annually mainly to discuss policy questions.

The police commissioner, key personnel, and other officers evaluate the Foundation's work as outstanding in meeting police department needs and priorities. Officers speak highly of the Foundation and express their desire to see a considerably higher budget for this independent body.

The police budget is too inflexible. Over 94 percent of it goes for personnel services (the cost of one patrol officer including deferred benefits is $28,000 annually); less than 1 percent for research; and the remainder for equipment, overhead, and other costs. The Foundation's budget is the prime source for high-risk projects and innovation. For example, the department would like to see more money used for management retreats (sensitivity training), development of model community councils and youth programs, and extensive promotion of the citizen block association concept.

There are other priorities too. Expressing confidence in the Foundation and its objectives, the police commissioner and staff have requested the Foundation to conduct an impartial opinion survey of police performance and effectiveness which would cost about $50,000.

Although Foundation projects are largely what the police department wants, the board is not afraid to get involved in controversial matters. It does not, however, involve itself in investigating the police department, organized crime, or similar matters in which a crime commission might engage.

The staff coordinates its ideas and proposals with other agencies, such as the city's Criminal Justice Coordinating Council, in order to avoid duplication and overlapping. In short, the Foundation attempts to do those things government will not or cannot do because of restrictive policies and budgets.

Indeed, Eliot Lumbard states that they do not favor receiving government funds for several prime reasons: (1) fear of restrictions on their activities; (2) belief that fewer donations would result if citizens felt the government was largely funding the programs anyway; and (3) that this is a citizens' group organized to aid a vital governmental service, not become another government expense. Furthermore, officials feel that too much staff time would have to be devoted to writing grant proposals and reporting. However, the Foundation seeks credibility and publicity from many sources so that it can effectively raise private funds in the future.

*Reasons for Success*

The success of the New York City Police Foundation is attributable to a number of factors. Chairman Lumbard enumerates the reasons:

1. We are effective because we have support from the very top of the police department.
2. We are influential because of an impartial board of recognized civic leaders sincerely interested in a better police department.
3. We are not in competition for power or status, preferring to remain in the background.
4. We do not try to run the police department or offer advice where we do not have the expertise.
5. We do not operate projects but merely help organize them and act as a catalyst.

*Activities*

Grants are made in such categories as citizen understanding and support, personnel development, law enforcement proficiency, management advancement, and scholarship development. The Foundation's ongoing programs are as follows:

1. *Public service information campaign.* A public service information campaign is now underway to heighten the community's awareness of the varied activities of the police department. It features 10- and 30-second television commercials, advertising car cards, and a special brochure entitled "The 100 Hats of Officer Jones." Over 1 million of the brochures, printed in both English and Spanish, are being distributed in banks, schools, supermarkets, and precinct station houses throughout the city. To assist the campaign, generous amounts of time were donated by advertising, public relations firms, printing unions, and others. The Foundation's auditor estimates that these free services and advertising time amount to about $250,000 a significant increase to the cost effectiveness of the Foundation's total budget.

2. *Public tours of police headquarters.* To promote police-community relations, public tours of police department headquarters are regularly scheduled. Tours chronicle the history of the department and feature a permanent exhibit of police memorabilia.

3. *Departmental workshops.* Experimental group seminars and encounter sessions designed to improve negotiation and mediation skills of police officers were funded in 1973. In 1973, the Foundation funded a series of 3-day human relations workshops for the discussion of black-white relations within the department.

4. *Narcotics arrest prevention program.* Through a grant to the Narcotics Arrest Diversion Program, narcotics education and prevention units have been placed in each precinct in the city for use by both narcotics officers and community relations officers.

5. *Management seminars.* To encourage exchange of ideas and procedures, a series of 3-day management seminars and conferences for police department personnel has taken place to discuss management problems and procedures. In addition, funds have been provided for attendance at police workshops in other cities.

6. *All ranks scholarship programs.* In April 1973, the former privately funded Police Scholarship Fund was merged into the Foundation. Under the merger agreement, new funds were earmarked for additional educational scholarships. A separate fund raising campaign will be undertaken for scholarships.

7. The Foundation is seeking new opportunities for the development of community and educational programs in the following areas:
   - Establishing management exchange programs between the police department and private industry
   - Preparing public information material for Civilian Radio Taxi Patrols
   - Sponsoring a series of interdepartmental seminars on attitudinal issues

8. The Foundation is acting as a catalyst for a review of the entire police-community council program.

Numerous grants and projects were undertaken by the Foundation from 1971 to 1973. These included such things as youth awards for Policemen's Basketball League, purchase and use of camping equipment, narcotics education and prevention, police training and research, police olympics, workshops and retreats, surveillance units for the police department, and police scholarships.

*Observations*

The New York City Police Foundation is performing a valuable community service by filling a budgetary gap which the New York City Police Department largely would not be able to do. Most important, it is performing a catalytic function for innovation and is acting as a buffer to keep the police department out of the business of public fund raising, which frequently leads to misunderstanding or worse.

It is unfortunate that the police department has been unable to budget funds for flexible and innovative types of projects. On the other hand, some of these projects are probably best funded by an independent group; furthermore, there is great merit in getting private citizens involved in the workings of the police department. Fund raising and setting project priorities are two such ways.

**Public Funding versus Private Funding.** A good deal of the projects funded by the Foundation could be funded by the police department. Public tours, brochures, narcotic kits, training programs, research seminars, management retreats, and a number of other projects eventually could and should find their way into the police budget. Most of these would be highly beneficial additions. Of course, this catalytic function is one of the prime purposes of the Foundation.

Other projects might best be undertaken by a private organization. Participation in police olympics, buying used taxicabs, funding neighborhood patrol groups, paying for the unusual entertainment of visiting officials, and granting awards and scholarships all appear to be more suited for private edeavor. A public relations campaign and public opinion survey would certainly have greater credibility if they were not only conducted but also funded by an independent source.

It is in these latter areas particularly that the value of a group like the Foundation is so readily apparent. We are all familiar with the stringency of government budgets, the inability to take on new projects quickly, and the fear of using public money for things of which the taxpayer might not at first approve. The Foundation is willing to experiment, take on high-risk projects, and simply do those things which a police department might not be able to do with its own budget. The whole field of organizing citizen groups and developing neighborhood responsibility is one such area where flexibility and some independence from police control are necessary.

Government officials are constantly frustrated by the inflexibility of their budgets. The quick decisions made by a small staff of Foundation officials makes it possible to bring in unexpected dignitaries, conduct unforeseen studies, hold emergency retreats, start innovative youth programs, and act as the catalyst for many other projects.

**Effective Method of Operation.** There is much commendable about the Foundation's method of operation. Channeling private funds in an anonymous way (to eliminate possible police favoritism) and disbursing money by means of impartial review are desirable techniques. Although conflicts remain with a few firms that wish to receive credit for their contributions, the fact that they agree with the policy not to expect favors in return dissipates the possibility of corruption and influence.

Furthermore, combining funds in one source improves priority setting. This is not to say that the collection of funds through some other source such as the Chamber of Commerce would not have a similar effect. Yet the singular purpose of the Foundation in police assistance makes it a more appropriate vehicle for this.

There is another asset to the Foundation's method of operation. Since it does not perform as a crime commission or make investigations of the police, its goodwill and rapport with the police department are maintained, and as such it is probably better able to achieve improved police-community relations and increased police management efficiency and effectiveness.

# 8      Police and Community Planning

Most of the programs we have discussed have a place in both large and small police departments.

Police and city planning officials need to assess their own city's total crime prevention requirements; furthermore, community organizations should be involved in initial and continual planning stages. Evaluation of the incidence of crime, location, type, methodology, and other factors will provide information as to which programs are needed and in which sections of the city. It is the responsibility of the police department to gather and analyze crime data and pass this information on, so that community groups can help set neighborhood priorities and overall city goals and objectives. It is not enough that police officials alone be involved in planning; block leaders and other residents should also participate.

One of the most effective ways to achieve resident involvement is through police-community councils, beat committees, anticrime crusades, or commissions. Once the police department has outlined the essential elements of a comprehensive crime prevention program, community workshops and neighborhood committee meetings should be held in order to reach agreement on community needs, priorities, and expenditures. These sessions should be held from the beginning of the planning stages and continue to be held periodically to review and update plans.

A typical police-community assessment might include the following elements and recommendations.

1. *Block clubs.* Establish block clubs in all sections of the city in order to get the maximum number of citizens involved and to discourage the criminal element from operating anywhere within the city limits.
2. *Federations of block clubs.* Utilize federations of block clubs in certain sections of the city where a multitude of clubs operate and where clubs wish to unite to carry on broader and perhaps more meaningful programming. The federations should be geared to assist and to help maintain weaker clubs and to work for more fundamental improvements in law enforcement.
3. *Block captains.* Select block captains and a deputy block captain for each block in the program. These leaders should be trained by the police department and also be capable of training and inspiring other block participants. Deputy leaders should always be available in case the block

captain moves from the area or otherwise cannot devote the necessary time. A well-organized block captain program should conserve police time and increase the department's ability to reach many more citizens.

4. *District leaders.* Appoint resident volunteers and police officers to head up each district for purposes of coordinating and stimulating block leadership. Civilian leaders could also be members of federations or areawide police-community councils.

5 *Special community police unit.* Establish a special police unit to promote and maintain volunteer block clubs and crime prevention projects. This unit may be located in the patrol division or in police-community relations. Location is less significant as long as beat patrol officers are assigned to meet and work with block clubs directly. Special police units should not be used as buffers between the regular police officer and the community. These units should be designed to get all officers fully involved with the community, coordinate projects, analyze data, organize property identification programs and home security, prepare newsletters and crime prevention pamphlets, provide speakers, and promote community involvement on radio and television.

6. *Community walks.* Encourage community walks in all sections of the city as part of the program for federations and other community improvement and crime prevention organizations. Walks can discourage the criminal element and increase sense of community and concern for lowering the crime level. Freon horns and whistles can be used as part of this program.

7. *Mobile patrols.* Start civilian mobile patrols in sections of the city or county where volunteers are highly motivated to perform this service. Patrols are especially useful in high crime areas, large parking lots, shopping centers, transit stops, and other special locations. Among other organizations, federations and anticrime crusades ought to take the initiative in forming mobile groups.

8. *Use of existing private vehicles.* Use existing business and government mobile units (radio- and non-radio-equipped) as eyes and ears for the police. Taxi associations, trucking firms, and city and county government departments can all be solicited and trained in how to watch for and report crime. Citizen radio mobile groups (those already licensed by FCC) should also be organized in crime prevention.

9. *Employee protection.* Organize employees who work late at night to assist each other. Techniques can include the buddy system, special transportation, increased police surveillance, special identification, and other protective methods. Employers or unions are well suited to organize this type of operation.

10. *Protecting children.* Organize PTA and other parent groups in each school district into crime prevention parent safety leagues. Adults should

patrol with older children. Window decals should be used to let children know they can use the identified homes for protection and shelter.

11. *Youth patrols.* Employ and train youths with special federal and state employment funds to put them into useful work, such as youth crime prevention patrols near schools, vacant property, parking lots, youth "hand-outs," concerts, and special events. Former delinquents under rehabilitation may also serve in patrols.

12. *Paid and unpaid civilians*

    *a. Auxiliary police.* Organize an auxiliary police force to assist in various police functions and to reduce crime efficiently and productively by making use of large numbers of volunteers who want to help but can only do so on a part-time basis.

    *b. Community service officers.* Utilize the community service officer program for those people who wish to advance through the police department ranks and to fulfill special assignments in administration, crime prevention, and more socially constructed areas.

    *c. Paid civilians.* Compensate and utilize specially trained and uniformed, radio-equipped civilians to assist police as partners during high crime periods. These would be young and old, male and female workers who are highly motivated and talented but who could not ordinarily meet the qualifications for sworn officers and who wish to work only part-time and in the performance of limited duties. Local planners have to assess whether such paid civilians would dampen the interest of unpaid auxiliaries. If used in special ways, the two concepts can work side by side.

13. *Police-community councils.* Establish police-community councils in sections of the city where citizens are sufficiently interested in working with crime prevention problems and taking the time to meet and assist police and to improve their neighborhood. Expansion citywide should occur only after several councils have proved that they can be successful. In some jurisdictions neighborhood police-community councils are sufficient organizations; in others, a central council or committee composed of representatives of the neighborhood councils and crime prevention groups should also be considered to deal with citywide crime problems and to act as coordinator of local crime prevention efforts.

14. *Anticrime crusade.* Encourage an anticrime crusade group to deal with problems related to the total criminal justice system. The initiative for this may come from the police department, Chamber of Commerce, League of Women Voters, Urban League, or other civic groups. The crusade should promote the idea of block clubs and police-community councils, as well as other crime prevention techniques.

15. *Private funding assistance.* Private businesses and civic and community groups should seek to establish a private tax-exempt foundation or

funding source to assist the police department in special projects and studies and to provide a noncontroversial source for the collection of funds which benefit police. This is particularly necessary in those cities where grave questions have arisen over the police department collecting funds for its own benefit.

## Comment

The ability and willingness for Americans to tolerate high levels of crime is astonishing. Perhaps it is because they have felt that they, personally, can do little about it. But the foregoing programs provide opportunity for citizens of all ages and income to participate in crime prevention.

Too often, the attitude of citizens has been to let government employees solve all the city's problems and to let them alone improve services. However, many of the cities are deteriorating, and problems are increasing. In the past few years, community councils and other techniques of decentralization have been used to help solve urban crises. Many of these projects have been effective and continue to operate. It is this same climate which has spilled over into law enforcement and has tenaciously held on in many communities. But this new spirit needs continual encouragement and signs that it is succeeding.

To a large extent law enforcement officials themselves have discouraged citizens from getting actively involved in stopping crime for fear that some innocent person might get hurt. Also some citizens are concerned that active participation may bring charges of spying or informing on one's neighbors. Such attitudes have hurt neighborhood involvement programs. Despite these negative inclinations, recognition of the importance of citizen participation remains, and many community-minded vitally concerned individuals are making sure that it succeeds.

The thousands of block clubs, neighborhood-oriented team-policing programs, citizen patrol groups, and other special citizen efforts for street and home security are indicative of the new concern. Almost every large city and county has some community-oriented project, while some are still afraid to promote active resident involvement. But police chiefs from almost every city surveyed praise and welcome citizen involvement, attributing crime reduction in specific areas to it. When crime drops in half or reverses itself on blocks where community groups function and work closely with police, it is difficult to argue against its effectiveness. This is what has happened in many jurisdictions. Results have been sufficiently successful to recommend that other communities organize and promote crime prevention projects.

As we have previously noted, the solutions to crime are complex, debatable, and sometimes remote. However, it appears that not much meaningful will ever be done about reducing crime without the active concern of all citizens. Responsible individual citizens will have to take the lead in setting up ways to to get residents involved, and simultaneously police and other city officials will have to understand citizen involvement, encourage it, and provide some resources and incentives to keep it going. The law-abiding, constructive nature of the programs described here is a good way to proceed.

## About the Author

**George J. Washnis** is president of the Project Development Center of Washington D.C. and was director of municipal studies for the Center for Governmental Studies, Washington D.C. for five years. He has served as chief administrative officer for the city of East S. Louis, Illinois for seven years; assistant city manager for Evanston, Illinois; and held two managerial positions in private industry. He received the Masters of Governmental Administration from the Fels Institute, Wharton School of Business Administration, University of Pennsylvania. His earlier publications include MUNICIPAL DECENTRALIZATION AND NEIGHBORHOOD RESOURCES (Praeger Publishers, 1972) that was chosen as a selection of the Library of Urban Affairs book-of-the-month club; and COMMUNITY DEVELOPMENT STRATEGIES (Praeger Publishers, 1974) that is perhaps the most comprehensive analysis of the Model Cities experience. He was also a contributing author to CITIZEN PARTICIPATION IN URBAN DEVELOPMENT (Learning Resources Corporation, 1974).

## DATE DUE

| | | | |
|---|---|---|---|
| SEP - 5 1990 | | | |
| APR 1 0 1996 | | | |
| | | | |
| | | | |
| | | | |
| | | | |
| | | | |
| | | | |
| | | | |
| | | | |
| | | | |
| | | | |
| | | | |
| | | | |
| | | | |
| | | | |